The D

MW01600579

My Stories and Personal Views on Belly Dance

By Leyla Najma

Copyright

Additional Resources

Here's a list of other Belly Dance resources you can click on and check out.

- <u>Online Belly Dance Classes w/Leyla at Belly Dance Village</u>
- <u>More Belly Dancing Articles on Leylas Blog</u>
- <u>Belly Dancing Leyla Style Mobile App</u> – On Amazon for Android
- Belly Dancing Leyla Style Mobile App on <u>iTunes for iPhone and iPad</u>
- Belly Dancing Leyla Style Mobile App on <u>Google Play</u>

Table of Contents

Introduction - Ode to a Belly Dance Family

"Families are always in the details of dancers movements. Love, passion, anger and laughter, are the descriptive ways we bring to life...our lives."

There are two kinds of husbands in the world, the average husband and then the Belly Dance husband. To be a Belly Dance husband takes commitment, tenacity, patience and courage. Multiple things happen in relationships with belly dancing; they are called coins, fringe, costumes and bling. Coins jingling to beats and clatter of a variety of sounds become the norm. Life doesn't exist outside the studio because the studio invades the hearth and heart of women all over the world. Either Belly Dance husbands understand this or they find they are competing with an arch-rival with super heroine powers. This is what sets belly dance husbands apart from other husbands, because they understand that the perks and fringe benefits out weigh any problems, drama or chaos that tags along.......well almost!

Sometimes, I feel a little guilty regarding my dance career because my obsession with belly dance has literally taken over my life, family, career and marriage. It's nothing that I planned on happening when I first started on my belly dancing path. It slowly took hold of me and enveloped all my senses to a point that I became a belly dancer by osmosis. So this is where my husband, Daniel comes in. He took my hand, jumped in and we haven't looked back since!

My daughter Savanah is my eyes when I can't see and she knows belly dance and all that comes with it. Being raised in a belly dance world has made her a young woman of the world, an aficionado of dance and astute in the diversity of cultures. She is one of my greatest advocates and without her honesty and support my dancing wouldn't be what it is today. Seeing her in the audience is one of my greatest joys in life, because the reflection looking back at me is always that of love, support and admiration. She is the wings beneath my feet and my fresh air of creativity.

The best part about belly dance for me has been the moments of empowerment I have shared with her or the insecure moments my career choice occasionally brings my way. Belly dance has helped both of us see each other in a way that allows us to be human with each other. I see perfection in my daughter and she reminds me every day how lucky I am she is in my life!

So I dedicate this book to my family because thanks to them I am honest, grounded, and for the most part sane. But best of all they take me as I am, and as a woman I couldn't ask for more!

Acknowledgements

I want to thank Daniel and Savanah who helped edit this book and put up with me during the final months of putting it all together. This definitely was a family affair!

Leyla Najma

1 - The Impassioned Years

"When passion is mixed in with a woman's objective to become successful the world becomes her accomplice and witness."

As a little girl my life changed forever one fateful morning years ago when I was six. I watched belly dancers on TV and knew from that moment on life would not be the same. Eyes glued to the TV screen and cereal coming out of my mouth, I gazed longingly as each dancer wove her magical spell on the TV screen. They were ethereal beings and everything I imagined what women should be. I saw myself wearing those beautiful costumes, the envy of all my friends. So with a grin and sigh I decided at that moment belly dancing was for me and I marched into the kitchen and informed my mother that I was going to be a belly dancer when I grew up. Being the good Catholic mother, she informed me that I didn't know what I was talking about and of course I couldn't be a belly dancer. I had a frown on my face which cost me a scolding and I was sent to my room a little more humbled and determined.

The belly dancing fascination never left me through out my childhood but it wasn't until I was sixteen years old, that I saw belly dancing again at a Greek Festival in my hometown of Albuquerque. I thought my heart was going to leap out of my chest, and it was all I could do just to stand there and watch the dancers. I had such a longing to get up on the stage and perform with them. There was a part of me that knew how to dance like them but my every day reality reminded me this was not true.

Have you ever felt something so strong that you were incomplete if you didn't do it or see it again? This is the way spirit tells us what we must do in life, and spirit will keep at us until we either do something about it or let it fade away. When we let our desires fade away, apart of us goes with them.

With my background growing up Catholic, the opportunities for learning belly dance didn't present themselves to me until I left home. The intense emotions stayed with me and as fate would have it, I finally faced my desire and started on my belly dance quest. In this case I started dancing in my early twenties. I ate, drank and slept belly dancing, disregarding anything else except for riding my horses and working cattle. Talk about two extreme identities; they were at opposite ends of the spectrum but to tell you the truth I wouldn't have had it any other way. I loved telling people that I both belly danced and worked cattle. Just the reaction out of people alone was worth saying it along with made up stories about how I would ride my horse to our camp site and belly dance the night away in front of our campfire. In my minds eye this is what I did, it all took place and sometimes it was hard to know the difference between reality and fantasy.

One thing I knew for sure, one day I would be dancing on stages in front of big crowds. Throughout the years I have realized that my fantasies helped me keep my desires in the forefront instead of the back burner of life.

Thank goodness for those magical feelings, because in reality, training and practicing are the only ways to get to that magical belly dancing goal. This is the part I didn't really think about and when I had really long days working cattle the last thing I wanted to do was practice. It's amazing what the mind can do to you when you're tired. It can pit one identity against the other, causing bickering and fighting. I can't really say that my two identities liked each other, they tolerated one another. Both aspects completed me though, because I wanted to be a cowgirl as much as I wanted to be a belly dancer.

Desire can be a very powerful tool because it doesn't allow the words "I can't," overwhelm us, therefore allowing us to become deaf to any words of discouragement. So both identities tolerated each other because they knew they were both my desires and neither of them had to compete with the other for my attention.

Continuing on my path was like an action adventure novel because there were so many unexpected surprises along the way. Not all of them were pleasant, and there were a few occasions where my mouth dropped open and life started to teach me my lessons, in ways I never dreamt of. And did I mention the part about not telling my parents that I was learning how to belly dance? Hmmm well this was the good Catholic girl in me, I thought. At the time, in my minds eye, I knew that the day I became famous they would have no other choice but to accept what I did. Unfortunately this was not convincing enough even for me, so I thought maybe I could use an alias while I danced. Little did I know at the time, that a part of dance is becoming someone else, a transformation into our dreams! It happens naturally, you become not only an alias to yourself but unrestrained from life itself. Dreams and fantasies of stardom took a toll on me and for awhile, everyday living became just a blur that was unless I was on my horse.

I have often wondered how people could go to work and accept a mediocre job, especially since there is so much creativity that pops and bursts out of us. In our acceptance of the need to make a living we can forget how to live. I went the mediocre path occasionally when I thought that dance was just an illusion. It's almost like a ping pong match goes on inside, until finally one side wins. As women we look for emotional well being in the movements and gestures of life, so how is it that a decision to become the end result of our goals and aspirations can be so confusing and difficult? The beginning years can yoyo a dancer into a raving lunatic, because our society tells us that as women we cannot be selfish and do anything for ourselves. Belly dance has the tendency to whisper in our ears that when we are happy and on stage, sharing our joy to the masses, we are the mirror opposite reflecting back the selfless women that we are. But convincing myself of this in the beginning years was hard. My surroundings became my first obstacle in the beginning years, only because the people around me told me there was no way to make a living dancing, and that I should be realistic instead of being naïve and impractical. Adding to this I became the second obstacle, because I listened to them.

Time seems to be on our side, and if we didn't have her, there would be fewer belly dancers on the loose. Eventually, most of us give in to our passion, and we finally accept the fact that we are belly dancers through and through. I really believe magic happened for me, because when I finally focused on my dance path, everything fell into place. Well ok, once it fell into place I did a lot of tripping over myself. Thank goodness through my struggles, my family and friends opinions changed from negative to a slight positive. This is where we intend what we want and people eventually move along with us in the same direction or they go their own way.

My journey started off in Austin, Texas with my first long weekend belly dance workshop. I didn't know what I was in for, and I found that those magical feelings I had inside, hid from me behind closed doors that were locked and sealed out of fear. The dance instructor was Horacio Cifuentes, who was and is a masterful dancer with a drill sergeant type of motivation. This was my first workshop and it was an eye opener. By the end of the weekend I felt like I had gone through a rite of passage, with a bit of boot camp put in for good measure! Unfortunately the annoyance of everyday reality showed its ugly head and I experienced for the first time mean spirited dancers. A few who didn't know it was my first belly dance workshop, felt it necessary to say, "Honey, this dance isn't for you." They assumed I was the cowering type, shying away from their negative words. Thank God my Scottish side is as stubborn as the wind. I realized, that negative experience was a reminder that the real world was also apart of my dance world. I felt like reality bit me in the "you know where" and to tell you the truth I would have preferred a warning with a nibble. Every time I think of those women to this day I smile, because little did they know they were the catalyst that catapulted me towards my belly dance path. Magic turned into pure determination, and I realized there are certain types of reality that seep in if you aren't careful. So if people become lemons turn them into lemonade or even better a margarita with a twist of lemon.

In the beginning of my belly dance quest, I couldn't find a belly dance teacher for at least two years. Finally, my searching led me to a wonderful dancer named Dina, who took me in and started teaching me the fundamentals of belly dance. As most beginners I was hungry for every move she taught, and had such enthusiasm, that at times I could tell she felt a little overwhelmed. Dina's heart was on the stage and after about 6 months of teaching me the basics, she told me our lessons were coming to an end. She felt she had started me on my path and that was enough. My heart dropped a little, because I knew this meant I was again, back to square one with my search for another dance teacher. Thankfully Dina directed me to my next teacher Sakti Rinek, who was and still is a great inspiration and motivator in my dance journey. Sakti shared every move with me, and she didn't hold back in helping me to become a well trained performer. As much as I enjoyed learning from Sakti, I realized with trepidation that because Sakti was an entertainer, my time with her was also going to be limited because of her traveling. So you can imagine my surprise when Sakti invited me to go to Egypt with her in the early 90's. Accepting Sakti's invitation redirected my belly dance journey onto a spiritual quest that to this day, has changed my life forever. With a wink of an eye, Sakti somehow knew.

Months later, being back on the ranch, I remember, the feeling of accomplishing a group of moves, and wanting someone there who understood, clapping and yelling along with me. There is no better feeling in the world than to be with people who understand what it takes to belly dance. Sometimes our families can be happy for us, but they don't always understand the tenacity it takes to do it. I remember one time, I was finally able to do a group of combinations, and there was nobody around except for my horses, goats, geese and chickens. I was actually practicing outside in front of them. As I was yelling and jumping up and down the horses started to run, the chickens and geese started to squawk around me and my goats were kicking up in the air. It was a pretty funny moment, one that I will always remember. On another occasion, I was practicing outside by the horse pasture, when my draft horses thought they should come on over and get their daily scratching. They came right up to me, sticking their big heads in my way, assuming a pat on the head was more important then whatever I was doing. They always won in the end, because they would crowd around me to the point I had no room to dance.

There was something else that came up within the first year that nobody told me about, which was the fervent need to prove my dancing was not just a hobby but something I really wanted to do. I'm not saying that every dancer out there wants to make a living solely with dance, especially factoring in that many forms of dance take up hours in a day, rehearsing and training. Belly dance like any passion, can consume so much time that it's easy to forget about time all together. This is unfortunately where arguments lurk, especially if your partner or spouse doesn't understand the commitment and dedication it takes to become successful. This wasn't what I envisioned when I started to belly dance, and to tell you the truth, it's the part of the reality of the dance that can be a setback if you let it. Early on most dancers learn that disillusionment and frustration become a common element mixed in with impassioned and frantic emotions. They merge together, creating moments of pure dramatic outbursts that become a part of our dance persona. The only guides we really have are those magical feelings that stay with us no matter what happens or who we become, meaning the drama queens in us are created along the way.

Even belly dance itself can take a beating after awhile, because it's so easy to hear about the drama and gossip that is created by women, and what's worse is how their targeted issues affect the dance community as a whole. It can be fun and interesting to watch first hand how dancers at studios, venues and workshops demonstrate their drama queen personas. The first time I saw how brutal women could be in this dance field was in a workshop in Dallas, I attended a few years into my dancing. One woman was a vendor and she came uninvited to the workshop and show. The workshop sponsor was very upset and arguments could be heard with hotel management eventually being called in to take care of the problem. It was sad to see the beauty and magic of the dance become tainted with the depressing reality of life that we were all trying to get away from for what felt like was only a brief reprieve from our busy lives.

As my dancing slowly progressed, I was asked to perform for the first time, in a student recital, even though I was not apart of the studio. When I arrived, I received my first lesson in dressing room etiquette or the make believe version. Side glances, rolling eyes and the whisperings of a select united front along with silent daggers being thrown occasionally was only the beginning. Women have a very unique way of telling each other how they "really" feel, by the shallow polite dialogue they have with each other. I understood this in my later years only because, sometimes I was apart of that shallow chatter. I have always questioned this type of etiquette because I would rather deal with the dead silence of valid feelings than wasted time on trivial niceties that mean nothing and are false.

When I took my dance experiences home with me and gradually absorbed them all, it became apparent that this dance form was not as magical as I had once thought it to be. I would liken it to a fairy tale story of lolly-pops and roses which was naïve and unrealistic. And as this reality set in I knew that our dance community wasn't any different than the real world. In truth we are real women dancing together in a real world and my naïve wonderland way of thinking finally faded away within the first five years.

This understanding replaced my original, youthful way of thinking, because dance truly comes from within and those magical feelings are the result of our connection to the Universe, not the drama that can unfold around us. The key is to make sure that issues don't sever this link.

So many women come into belly dance because they are facing issues and problems on the home front or work place. Belly dance can become the remedy of choice or a band-aid that only covers the deeper issues. It just depends on what the intention of the dancer is. Belly dance is a natural therapy for the mind, body and soul but I have seen it used as a superficial cover up that only touches the surface of issues, never healing the deeper problems.

I worked with a wonderful dancer in my early years that was the antithesis of her belly dance image. The dance seemed to ease her pain, but I couldn't really understand how she could separate herself from her dance persona and stay sane. The two were extreme opposites. Perhaps her insanity is what kept her going, because in the real world sanity and insanity can become a blur pulling the two together. What the audience sees up on stage isn't always what is backstage in the dressing room. As I learned, we can become the shadow of our own self loathing all the while dancing on stage with confidence and practiced proficiency.

I thought, belly dancing was an escape from troubled times. In reality it magnified my life lessons some of which I didn't want to deal with and others I didn't even know I had. The innocent passion that I started out with turned into a seasoned participation, and observation of a dance form that took hold of me and wouldn't let go. To say belly dance was my fix was an overstatement, and to say I was addicted was an understatement. Belly dance was my right of passage from the innocent woman that I was, to the more mature woman that I have become. I am wiser and wearier of my path, yet at the same time, I can't wait to see what's around each bend in the road. Walking cautiously on my path is a lesson that even to this day trips me up because I always want to run or skip to the next bend in the road instead of pacing myself.

Dance is to be celebrated so on occasion I jump for joy realizing that I can let go of any inhibitions limiting my choices, desires and dreams. Is this not the true source connection? The connection took my rose colored glasses off, and I realized that the enchanted experiences I had and the emotions I felt at specific times, were feelings of naïve expectations with no understanding to back them up. The connection helps create a way to understand each experience we have so we can see where we are in life. Because of this the magic bursts out of us and keeps us eager to walk the twists and turns of our dance path. We learn how to walk, step around and jump along the path and this amazingly is what makes the seasoned dancer. My passion for belly dance is as great today as it was in the beginning but with the obvious difference of an old school mentality. Now, my fire burns brighter and I have come to realize that it is my job and no one else's to keep my fires burning, not just brighter but emblazoned with life's experiences.

I must admit, the little girl eating her cereal, watching belly dance for the first time, is still within me. There is no blemish on her purist perspective, only the joy and love for a dance form that changed her life forever. She is not only me but I think she is all of us.

2- Keeping Your Self Identity

"Belly dance is a combined language that people understand without knowing why. It's primordial in visual appeal and instinctive in fantasy."

There are so many life lessons that transpire, which eventually shape who we are and transform how we think. Because of this, we live life from constant change and experiences that affect our emotional, spiritual, physical and mental well being. How we relate to other dancers says a lot about how well we are doing in our own lives. But ultimately what speaks volumes is how we see ourselves in the mirror and how we react to our reflection, skewed or unadulterated. Do we treat ourselves as well as we do others? Or are there hidden agendas, we hide behind even from ourselves? Self Identity evolves through accepting the truth about ones self and dancing without any apology or regrets. Within my first couple of years of dance, my self identity took a beating not because I was blind to myself, but because I saw myself through all my mistakes, wrong turns and floundering struggles with my dance.

Eventually at the 5 year mark, the dancer in me emerged and finally showed herself to the world. My identity was not all my own yet, but the end result of teachers I admired and befriended. At that point, my identity was influenced and molded by the styles and methods of a multitude of teachers. While this was a part of my learning process, I realized that I didn't own my dance yet. When we own our dance, we dance like no one else, staking claim to our reflection, becoming one with ourselves with the need to imitate someone else fading away.

Self Identity

As my awareness grew, I developed into a dancer that flourished, first in my observations of dancers and then with the many levels of training it takes to become the best. As I progressed through my classes and workshops, something interesting happened, I acquired combinations and gestures from the teachers I studied with but I didn't know what to do with them once I got them home. I saw how beautiful the moves looked on each instructor that I admired, but when I tried to move like them, I lacked the natural grace they had. In the end, I just didn't move like my teachers and there was a part of me that felt like I never would. I had to learn that the moves had to become a part of who I was first, and only then would they become "my" moves.

This meant that I could admire my teachers but at the same time separate my "identity" from them and dance the combinations my way.

The funny thing is, I didn't develop my own "identity" until I was dancing for about ten years and there were quite a few years that I danced without knowing who I was or that the dance had to come from within me. As a matter of fact, I

15

didn't know that it had to come from within me because I was too busy dancing outside of myself. It occurred to me I had a problem when a fan came up to me and said "I know you, you're what's her name?" They couldn't remember my name, which made me feel worse. I thought, if I am being mistaken for someone whose name nobody can remember, what does that say about me? I came home that night, and realized that I had to reinvent myself, and start to understand what I wanted from my dance.

Reinventing Myself

At the time, reinventing myself seemed like such a radical response but one that was necessary. Push came to shove because of an experience I had in Dallas, a few weeks later. I auditioned at a small restaurant, and was told by the owner, in a rude manner to go home and learn how to belly dance. I was dancing at other restaurants already so his attitude didn't compute, and for a minute I thought he was joking. That night, I went home knowing it was a harsh lesson to experience, but one I had to learn from and one that I have never forgotten. Ultimately, I knew there was some truth to his statement. That particular restaurant owner gave me a wonderful gift and opportunity, because he pushed me in the direction of self evaluation.

There were two roads that I could have traveled. One was to ignore his comment all together and continue on my path the way it was. The other was to change my dance style, resulting in a new me. Of course, the dancer in me was determined to prove the restaurant owner wrong, and show him I knew how to dance. Since I love a challenge, I decided to forge ahead, improve my dance and walk back into his restaurant for another audition.

The first step was to look in the mirror and to see what others saw when I danced, and then go back to square one. This was liberating because I worked from the inside out. I decided to do moves that only felt good in my body. Secondly, I decided to change how I put moves together and go outside the box of "safe" moves. I changed what was right for me and let go of ideas that just didn't fit me anymore. Every performer has her view of dance and as we learn, we need to decide what to keep and what to let go of and know that this is ok. I decided there were certain ways that I preferred to dance besides what I was told. So I decided to follow my instincts and not limit myself, going for my higher inspiration.

All of a sudden as a few months passed, a dancer emerged from within me that I hadn't seen before. I danced up to three hours a day and kept it up for about three months. You can imagine the restaurant owners face upon seeing me walk into his restaurant, asking him for another audition. He hesitantly told me to come back when he wasn't so busy. I smiled and told him I would be back the next day after lunch. The next day, I arrived with such enthusiasm and eagerness that at times I felt I was going to burst at the seams. I must admit this didn't happen during the first audition. I knew these new feelings added a spice to my dance that I didn't have before. As my audition started, my new dance persona emerged and took flight. After I was done with the audition, the restaurant owner smiled at me and said, "So you learned how to belly dance." I was hired that day.

Through this experience, I learned that the emotional state of a dancer is a key element in the success of her story telling. If we don't believe in ourselves we can't expect others to. The biggest let down for any audience is to see a dancer apologizing for being herself and for telling a story she doesn't believe in. That day I vowed to never dance without believing in myself or my dance.

"Self identity and self acceptance are the end result of a woman's style; it's her divine connection to the euphoric self" Leyla Najma

Student Growth

Years later when I opened up my own studio, I realized that it was crucial for my students to learn and develop their own identities. As teachers, we have to help our students understand that they come first and foremost to the studio to learn the dance form. It is up to them to eventually develop the movements into their bodies and once they do this, only then is the individual dancer born. I can remember students coming into my studio for exercise or companionship who had a glimmer of hope of what they would see or feel as they danced. I could see them search within themselves for what they had lost, or for what they hoped to find. As each student regained apart of herself she would change from; I will never dance publicly, to asking me months later, if there was a chance she could perform in the next show. Individual creativity unlocks the mind because it releases the restraints of our own self imposed conditions of how we allow ourselves to be. Dance frees the soul and the end result is always a feeling of being reborn. As a studio owner, watching the creative process work was priceless.

The most rewarding outcome for a teacher is to see the dancer emerge and transform within each student. Eventually, most students want to spread their wings and fly and true to form I have found this always happens at the one year mark. But because teachers are dealing with the students emotional self, certain situations can surface that can test a teacher's patience and regard for individual creativity. If a students self identity isn't allowed to emerge, one or two things frequently happened. Some students become dissatisfied with their teacher's knowledge or they volunteer their opinion without being asked.

A few questioned my combinations and technique but they didn't know enough to take their argument further. Sometimes the dancer would periodically emerge before the student understood how to fly. Since their feeling of self creativity is so powerful, it would put into question my teaching authority. Because of this, sometimes a student wouldn't listen to me and they would prematurely jump or fly away in defiance of my training. Since we are all learning how to walk our own path, I realized that they had to jump and I had to watch them either land on their own two feet or fall and pick themselves back up. I did this myself at certain periods in my dance career, and I feel even to this day that it helped me understand my path better and appreciate when the road was less rocky. To put it bluntly, It can be painful when we land on rocks. As a teacher, a helping hand makes the lesson less painful and humiliating because we can give our students the pill of compassion that makes it all the easier to swallow.

"We are not our age, we are a combination of lessons learned, not learned and repeated" Leyla Najma

I also went through moments of "identity crises" with a few of my teachers. You can only be a "star student" for so long. I felt that my ability wasn't being appreciated, and that they were acknowledging me only through their own accomplishments of teaching me. If I did a good job of dancing then that meant my teachers did a good job of teaching. After a while, I just wanted to do a good job of dancing based on my own perseverance and hard work. I have also known some dance teachers who found it easier to ignore the steps students and dancers took by keeping them on a derisory shelf called *amateur*. As time passed, I knew the steps leading me along my path, always helped me end up where I was suppose to be. I also enjoyed those stopping points where I rested and reevaluated my path.

For a long time, my fear was that I would end up being isolated and distrustful like some teachers. Then it occurred to me that everyone experiences dealing with their own fears of being replaced or forgotten. We can get so wrapped up in our own identities that we can't see past the illusion we have created, and it can eventually end up dominating our everyday life. The fear of being a *"has been"* can keep a well known dancer from seeing that it is okay to acknowledge dancers up and coming. One thing I have learned is that our self identity can be sealed tight as a drum in the beginning and through years of walking our path of unexpected curves, drops and steep inclines, it can loosen its grip and insecurities can seep in. As women we are scrutinized enough in society, so why is it that we do this to ourselves and others? It is also important to know that "self identity" can't be forced; it has to evolve along side with us.

At one particular workshop show I danced in, I went and sat down in the audience after my performance to watch a dancer perform a classical Egyptian piece. Through out most of the dance I saw what appeared to be a painful look on her face. At first, I thought something was wrong and I didn't know if I should get up and go backstage to tell someone. Towards the end of her performance, she smiled and I thought maybe I had just imagined it. When I asked her if she was feeling well, she said she was fine and then proceeded to tell me that she was really trying to show the audience how she felt about the song. I must have had a shocked look on my face because she asked me what I thought of her performance. I started to feel uncomfortable so I told her that she danced well because in truth she did. I just omitted the part about her painful expression, leading me to think she was ill.

Even though she tried to convince the audience that she understood the song, in the end, the forced expression on her face took away from her dance. It was a surprising lesson, because it became apparent that we really need to understand the different cultures in which we represent. When we try to emulate a song, we really need to bring it in and absorb it into our own experiences. We can't translate a song without understanding that our own identity has to have something in common with the words, otherwise we can end up confusing our audience or like in this case, lead them to think something is wrong. It is so important to bring life into movement in a believable manner, because if a dancer doesn't understand how to feel the music authentically, her audience will notice. Part of understanding our "self identity" is to understand the connection between the two cultures we absorb and eventually represent. When this happens we welcome our audience into our dance by showing them not only how we live life but how we understand life within other cultures.

The Costume and Style

The belly dance costume has so much to do with our self identity. In today's day and age, the belly dance costume has taken on drastic changes, that I never saw coming. It's no surprise that these changes occur from generation to generation, but it seems to me that the changes of today are a bit more drastic and dramatic, because belly dance is now integrated with other dance forms. Add younger women into the mix with older veterans and sometimes you have a never before seen cacophony. Women have an idealized way of looking not only at their own curves, but other women's curves. Those who put on their blinders can be at a disadvantage especially in a world that adores beauty. Being unrealistic is beside the point, because somewhere along the way I lost track of what I thought the true and defining image of a belly dancer really was. The younger generation of today came right in and didn't think twice when making themselves at home consequently creating a variety of styles that have blended cultures, dance forms and personal taste. It's like they knew exactly what they were doing and I have to admit I felt like I had missed the boat. Though I wasn't sure if I wanted to be in the boat, I realized that sometimes procrastinating can be costly.

Style plays a part too, because it's our signature detail that makes us who we are. One day, I was talking to a dance friend and we started chatting about the topic of style, and I realized that style is just another aspect of self identity. The younger generation came in knowing what they wanted and they knew how they wanted to look. This can be the icing on the cake because once we know who we are as dancers, and then we can pull in our style which helps create the finishing touches, completing our belly dance image. Yet there are women like myself, who didn't realize our style was the tip of the iceberg, especially with the endless choices of inspiration. Since we are learning a cultural dance form it's easy to see why we feel our style doesn't count, because we are learning not just dance but about cultures that represent different ideals, customs, traditions and outside influences.

The younger generation learned how to merge their own styles with the traditions of this dance form, without blinking an eye. This is interesting to say the least, because in some ways I am talking about two different types of style. Since style is a part of our self identity, I really think we make it more complicated than it needs to be. There is of course the different cultural styles of belly dance that appeal to women, and we find the style that fits us the best. I have watched many women, including my own students, instinctively pick their style of costume and dance without wavering from their desires.

As women define their style, they not only solidify who they are in everyday life but they give their dance persona a sense of value. Most women have a specific way they dress and certain mannerisms that make them stand out in a crowd. This doesn't go away just because they learn a new dance form. As a matter of fact, I believe that the allure of style is further enhanced because they have a new way to express themselves. When women see dancers who are accomplished, they see how comfortable they are in their own skin. Self confident enhances any performer's style to the point, the audience takes notice.

Style is a confidence that is connected to us by virtue of being born a woman. As the mass media has shown us, if we compare our style with other women, we place ourselves in a state of constant lack. A long time ago, I decided that no matter how far I would go in belly dance, I would keep my sense of self, thus keeping my self identity intact. Style that starts with how we feel about ourselves can visually be seen when we perform and express ourselves on stage. When a dancer is confident about herself and her dance, the end result is a comfortable glow that showcases her "natural" style.

Self identity evolves as our dancing evolves and our style just shows the world we understand who we are at any given moment. My self identity has become what it is today because I didn't give up on myself, and I realized that I am where I am because of my teachers and friends who supported me along the way. All of this support helped me evolve in my dance, and become an active member in my community, besides being okay with walking my path alone. It's almost like carrying everything you need with you, and being prepared for what life throws your way at a moments notice. It's the end result of confidence coming full circle with style as its companion and confidante.

"Style is a woman wearing a dress and making it her statement. It's in the attitude of a woman that finishes off the outfit so there is no imitation." Leyla Najma

Everybody has something to share in this dance form, which means that an open mind helps with the exchange of ideas, each generation brings with them. The silent knowledge of style and confidence adds that extra sparkle to our internal wardrobe that everyone wears when they are performing on and off stage. The best part, is even if the lessons of life evade us, we persevere wearing the truth of our understanding of what our self identity is. A confident dancer stands before her audience without regret or shame. Self identity and self acceptance are the end result of a woman's style; it's her *divine connection* to the euphoric self.

3 - A Common Diversity

"Creativity is not defined, it is lived."

Amazingly enough, with the crossing of time, life slowly prepared me for my future in belly dance, with a bolt from the blue. One lesson in particular that turned out to be an unexpected reality check, was that if you were any good, that wasn't a guarantee that you could get work. There is no rule of thumb that says, if you can dance, other dancers will ask you to be in their shows. Basically what I am saying, is that many a good dancer has gone to the way side, waiting for her chance to dance. This happens because our community has opinions on who they think are good dancers. It doesn't matter if you think you are good, other dancers may not agree, and there lies the problem.

Dance and Performing

I also realized quickly, that invitations to perform in shows depended on if you knew and got along with various studio directors. Dance in the end is about getting to know individual communities. Being a travelling belly dancer that magically appeared out of nowhere, and then, puff would vanish, didn't help me much. Women feel the need to be able to trust the dancers that are in their inner circle, and I found that repeatedly being the new girl on the block didn't garner me any camaraderie with anyone. It became clear, that if I was lucky enough to be in a community that liked me, then I was more likely to perform in shows. It was obvious that obscure locations offered no support or opportunities. This is part of the reality check that I experienced traveling and working cattle. Being stable was something I definitely had to work on. I loved the gypsy life, but there's a price you pay when you live life from one camp to the next.

Life taught me that the minimal amount of time I spent trying to get to know dancers was not fully welcomed because of the trust factor. In our dance world, women have a tendency to stay close to those who intimately share their lives, and dance together. I think in a way our dance pays a price for this, because new dancers will come in and create competitive troupes, dance venues, especially if they feel they are being left out. It's to be expected that dancers stay together especially with their creativity at stake. Each dancer has their own specifics on studio ethics and dance preferences.

Sometimes studios prefer "their way" sometimes shunning outside ideas, even if they seem like good ones. It's almost like studios are like a household with a particular fondness for their own creative process and preferences regarding who they choose to walk their dance path with. Specific ideas are usually already put into place, and the comfort level of expression is close knit. Understanding this makes us more compassionate to communities. As we make our own foot

I learned that experience comes with opinions and those opinions become life statements of what does and doesn't work. But a question arose from the depths of my mind that lingered with me for a long time, " Is this the building block of criticism?" What happens when we create a community that is critical of specific dance groups, dance styles, dance ability or dance venues? How healthy is the air we breathe in our environment, when we contaminate it with criticisms and censorship? Is this necessary or does it do the opposite, which is to clear the wheat from the chafe?

Dance Changes

As time progresses along two things happen for dancers, either they keep up with the changes or they look around scratching their heads asking, "Where am I?" Obviously, this has happened to me to such a point that it seems like all I do is scratch my head. If you are lucky enough to be in the group that has kept up, then you know where you are. But I'm in the group, where changes have occurred that I didn't necessarily care for. To tell you the truth, I'm dipping my feet in both pools because I kept up and than decided to slow my pace and stay behind. But sometimes when you walk behind a crowd, you can hear the echoes and whisperings of those walking ahead of you. It can be really interesting listening to the murmurs of chatter emanating from the wind.

I'll never forget a dance acquaintance of mine a long while back said most of the shows that she had seen up to that point were just horrible. Since I was in most of those shows, I was left wondering if this was her round about way of insulting me. I cut her some slack and decided she must have had amnesia when she was talking to me. With a blank stare, I let her think it didn't compute but it was tactless to converse about something like that in the first place knowing that I, along with many of her friends were in those specific shows.

Sometimes to be oblivious is a good thing but in dance it can become a major downfall, because dancers will talk gossip because it's in their competitive nature. A good example of this was at a concert that I performed at with a dance friend years ago. The concert director invited us to dance and requested that we perform to taped music. For some odd reason, the concert director thought I bullied my dance friend into performing to my preference in music. The night of the show after I arrived, she started to scream and yell at me infront of guests arriving in the front lounge of the hotel. The image of Medusa immediately came to mind because if looks could kill, I would have been dead. Come to find out my dance friend complained to her without me knowing it and made me look dishonest to the concert director. I learned that evening that even in our dance world of so called sisterhood, there is a competitive rivalry amongst dancers that can hinder any kind of unity you might have with each other. As for me, there was no saving grace with this concert director, and I was never sure what my dance friend wanted to accomplish, outside of making me look bad. Well...okay, that was obviously the reason.

Experience has taught me that looks especially packaged in a beautiful body can create a disadvantage when it comes to equal consideration. The world reacts differently to beautiful people. I experienced the other side of this coin when I was rehearsing with a dance friend, for a restaurant show we were doing together in Fort Worth, Texas. She was a very striking woman and when the band saw her walk into the room, they were mesmerized by her, and gathered around he, forgetting about me. After trying to figure out how to handle my predicament, I just started to laugh. After about twenty minutes of chitchatting, everyone started to gravitate towards the doors as if they were going to leave. I was surprised and concerned because we didn't rehearse yet. It became apparent my dance friend didn't feel like rehearsing, so the band was willing to call it a night. Perhaps I'm exaggerating a bit, but from back in the abyss I told them in a loud voice that I wanted to rehearse even if my dance friend didn't want to. All of a sudden, the band came out of their trance and I became visible in the room again. To this day I am so grateful that I spoke up, because the evening of our show I received accolades for my performance, one being the restaurant owner commenting it was the best performance he had seen me do. I restored faith in myself for speaking up during rehearsal, because even an invisible woman has a voice.

The Ideal Woman

As women do we look harsher on beautiful women because we feel they have an advantage over us, or do we help them become successful in our business because we want to see the symbol of our dance in a beautiful woman? Is our dance form really women friendly? When I say women friendly, I mean all types of women. Do we as women censor our own belly dance image without even knowing it?

Many women want to be well known but can they handle it if a dance friend gets there first? Women gage how they are doing by other dancers that are at their level of success. This is where criticism lurks in dark corners. You know what I mean, the eyes dart back and forth, side glances occur at an alarming rate, and the look of total antipathy comes across the face. Even if a dancer did well, the blur of aversion would keep another dancer from seeing a performance well done. Who at this point is at a disadvantage? This in particular occurs when the dance style is different from what a dancer prefers. Is there rivalry amongst dance styles? Let's be honest here, yes of course there is! With the different styles, follows change especially in the belly dance costume. Our belly dance costume is almost like a super heroine alter ego. Once we change into our costume, we become antithesis of our everyday mirror image.

When dancers perform together, the saving grace is how diverse we are, because there is no greater way to show an audience that we are from all walks of life, than when we are on stage together. How can we educate our audience on the diverse elements of our dance, if we can't accept the changes that are taking place in our dance world ourselves? At certain points within my career, I stuck to my guns regarding my view of dance, but I have come to realize that when I started out, I was a part of change; a change my generation brought with it. So are my feelings telling my age?

The Traditionalists and the Next Generation

There have been occasions when I felt like a fish out of water. For instance, I remember performing in a local show called, Oriental Potpourri in my hometown of Albuquerque. We were all required to be on stage together, and just as the curtain was about to open, it hit me that I was the only cabaret dancer on stage with tribal dancers. I looked to my right and then to my left, and I was overwhelmed by the kaleidoscope of color. It was the most amazing sight I can remember seeing, and I could only imagine the gasps from the audience upon seeing the array of color unfolding before their eyes. I knew from this particular show, that change had already arrived. The troupe dynamic is very popular now especially with their edgy tribal vibe. Todays dancers are willing to take more risks, and push the traditionalist's boundaries. Each generation has to make their own way, and as they do there will be dancers wanting to keep the old ways in place by pushing back. It's obvious that I am one of those dancers pushing back.

Solo or Troupe

Though, I love to watch troupes perform, solo performing is my first love. For me, it has been a privilege to be a solo performer, because it takes tenacity and bravado to get out in front of people. Once we offer our creativity to the masses, it is like being naked, because we are being judged on our ability to entertain and perform. Imagine going out on the dance floor, right after a troupe has performed with unison, grace and perfect timing. Not only does a solo performer's soul have to be willing to take up the whole stage, she has to become her dance. If dancers don't put censorship on their artistry and try to define themselves, their dance will grow in the way that it needs to. When dancers submit to their dance, then the audience sees who they really are and once their comfort level relaxes, the audience relaxes with them.

As a solo performer, I have found that I don't have more to prove; it's just fun to embellish on my own work of art by allowing my choreography to be overstated or understated according to the audience's response. It's more fulfilling for me to allow the audience to help me finish my dance. It becomes something unexpected even to me.

The Creative Oops

I have always wondered where does tradition and change exist together, and the conclusion I came to was unanimous, it is on the stage. It's the one place where dancers won't criticize each other because in a way, it's almost taboo. The stage makes everyone equal to each other, and if dancers see success around them, what is there to criticize? Creative expression is usually judged harsher by our own insecurities but than I've heard stories of inappropriate themes and choreographies in shows. Since we live life in so many different ways, it is bound to happen that creative expression gets caught in the middle of individual principles and values. Shock value isn't usually what people go to a dance show for, especially if they are bringing family and friends along with them. I remember being a part of a show where a dancer had a flashlight and her dance was created around turning her flashlight on and off. I didn't get it and neither did the audience, but she had a really good time which I have to admit left me perplexed. So even an idea can cross the line of the bizarre in effect leaving an entire audience with mixed feelings. A wacky idea or experience can turn an awkward moment, into an embarrassing and unintended blunder that is immortalized in photos and videos. I know this one well!

A good example of one of my blunders happened at a restaurant here in my in Albuquerque. My predicament started out with the owner of the restaurant yelling at me through the bathroom door, "Your music is starting!" "Oh no", I thought to myself as I walked out of the bathroom. As I walked out, unbeknownst to me, my skirt was tucked into my underwear. I danced to part of my first song with my right cheek showing to everyone. I did feel a breeze, but then I was doing turns so I thought it was normal. One of the waitresses cracked up laughing and came over and pulled my skirt out. "Thank God!" Fortunately there were no close friends visiting or dancers giggling at me giving me that, I'm so embarrassed for you look. The wait staff and customers were bad enough. Life can be a comedy where the jokes on you.

Self Respect and Rockin the Boat

I had thought that if dance communities pulled together to create a world that makes each and every one of us feel safe, then our diversity would make sense to everyone it touches. In the end, I realized that it isn't just diversity but common courtesy that we need to work on. An example of bad behavior that has stayed with me all these years is embodied in a dancer who produced workshop shows in the Dallas area years ago. I had attended at least six workshops she produced, which was my way of learning my art form and supporting my community. But every time I saw this woman, she never remembered my name and was aloof with me to the point of being rude. I remember the last time I went to one of her workshops, I had hoped for a more gracious encounter but inevitability was greeted by her usual rude self. I was not the only one she behaved this way with, so I asked myself an important question; with so many workshops to attend elsewhere, why was I supporting her bad behavior? I also had to wonder what had happened to my self respect.

Perhaps self identity and self respect are closer than we think. Furthering this observation, I realized self creativity that is selfish or blind to the comfort of others is another major problem here. We live in a world where we want to toot our own horn, but we need to understand that we also fit in with a community that symbolizes all of us. I am a part of a diverse multitude of dancers who are constantly bringing in different views of the world. Perhaps with the variety of world views, we can figure out ways that bring the best out in our communities. Sometimes, we allow bad behavior to happen because we don't want to rock the boat but then you have to figure out if you are in the right boat. Since a hodgepodge of beliefs regarding our dance have been around for years, it became clear to me that bringing together the old and the new would create a potpourri of innovative ideas that would compliment each other without clashing.

There's a quote that says; *"A critic is a man who knows the way but can't drive the car."* For some women traveling on their dance path, knowing the way seems easy, almost self guiding. As for myself, it never occurred to me that getting lost was ever going to be part of my dance experience. As belly dancers we have more of an adventurous spirit to us than most, so finding our own way seems to be apart of the belly dance experience. From my perspective, belly dancers are always looking for new experiences; in essence roads less traveled. But no matter what direction or fork in the road, the goal is the same, to reach our dreams and aspirations. We represent ideas, experiences and history from all walks of life besides our own. So when we dance together this reflects back to the audience that we are a unique brew called diversity.

If our self identity is based on experiences through out our lives, then I often wonder why belly dance isn't considered a more complex art form. We are looking at sensuality, sexuality, relationships, self respect, and a multitude of other aspects of which we are as women, tied up into one specific dance form. It's no wonder you never know what you will experience backstage or onstage. What this really means is that we have always been diverse maybe we just didn't know it. The funny thing is, diversity has been the one aspect we all have in common. The important thing is to remember to look out the window and enjoy the view. Just remember to watch out for the occasional bug flying by.

4 - Dancing to Your Own Tune

"No one follows somebody else's tune, only because it isn't in our nature to follow what we can't hear."

Sometimes, this dance form can cause even the most seasoned dancer to doubt herself. It's not necessarily dancers questioning their ability, but the false pretenses that reality can throw their way. The problem is, every once in awhile we believe in the shallow promises that the limelight can offer us. I have seen the allure of this dance form bring dancers to great highs and without a moments notice, drop them to their knees. I am definitely including myself in this one.

The Alter Ego

This dance form can seem misguiding, because it can lead us to believe in things that ordinarily we wouldn't. Self discovery isn't an easy road to travel, especially when dealing with the enticement of costumes, music and performing. It's easy to veer off our course in this dance. It can also make any dancer feel like she is going in a multitude of directions at the same time. For this reason, it can be hard to distinguish between where we are going versus our original goals. Sometimes, we have to step back and take a good look at what we want from this dance, in order to keep our original intention.

Lurking in the darkest reaches of a woman's mind, is a menacing, prejudiced opinion of herself. Taking a dip in a hidden pool of self doubt seems to be in our nature, because it invites us to scrutinize ourselves. Whispers escape us, surrounding us, speaking in words that only we can hear. It's not so much we compare ourselves to other dancers, we compare ourselves to the image we have in our head. If our dance doesn't look like what we imagine, we justify what we lack, by creating an alter ego. A major problem that can come from this is when we allow our alter ego to take over all communication. The reality is that some dancers don't want to face the reality of their dance personas limitations. Unfortunately, most of us have come across dancers who were so busy living through their alter egos that they made it hard to get to know them.

It's pretty much a given, that we slip up and share a little unwanted diva, every now and then. It's almost like we create a self made deformity that at days end, is looking back at us, every time we look in the mirror. We can only deny our self created deformity to a point, before we eventually break down at the most inappropriate of times. We don't lose our tempers or fall apart on a directors timing; this isn't life and it isn't realistic. We pour ourselves a dose of our self inflicted inadequacy instead of just dancing, for no other reason then to dance. Our original passion becomes obsolete because for some reason, dancers turn their insecurities into irrational fears. I've learned to stay the course by believing in my dance and understanding where my rhythm comes from. By doing this, I can dance to my own tune without worrying about any self made constraints.

The Emotional Onion

Sometimes dancing to our own tune can make us feel alone, because in order to dance, we have to be willing to take a risk that we can actually dance. Life will give us what we ask for, including what we don't want. The irony for some dancers is that we unintentionally include what we don't want into our requests, or meditations. Life's' indifference doesn't question our request; it will give us what we ask for without hesitation. The lesson with anything we ask for is to understand we sought it out even though we choose to be oblivious to our own request. This is the part of life that can really trip us up. So if we want to create our own harmony, we have to sort through what it is we really want versus what we habitually and mindlessly ask for. The alter ego can easily come in and state its case for a variety of wants and needs that seem important to us at the time. But eventually if we look ahead of our own agenda and peel away issues and problems, the end result will truly be what we want leaving the alter ego no other choice but to fade away. Unfortunately, my alter ego tries to make an appearance every now and again. I know if I look at what I really want out of life versus an impulsive desire, I can usually tell if it's really me or the alter ego making her rounds.

I have found that my emotional onion is bigger than I thought it was, because as I have peeled away old lessons and problems, I have noticed that sometimes it doesn't look like I've made any progress. And to be honest, sometimes I'm still a yo-yo. As we go through different lessons and experiences, there seems to be a crossroads at the end of each path that defines if we benefited from our lessons, or caved in to the feelings of failure. If we don't get the jest of life's lessons, it will offer up two signs, one pointing us back to square one and the other telling us, we can pass. A person can only go back to square one so many times, so I did the unthinkable, I said no. It must have been the belly dancer in me because I decided sometimes the lesson is knowing when to say no.

Since everyone is following their own tune, I wonder if part of the problems we all encounter, stem from the fact that some dancers don't want to acknowledge their contemporaries individual tunes. The biggest problem I see in this business is the fact that some dancers don't even want to acknowledge another dancers individual ability. They basically "tune" out to anything other then their own wants and needs. The alter ego can only go so far, because in the end whether we acknowledge it or not, life throws us unpredictable curve balls. So my lesson has been to understand that my dancing is a personal expression of how I hear music. But our common goal as a community, is to express our creativity together, enjoying varieties of interpretations along with our own.

Understanding How to Listen

Sometimes how a person interprets the music they hear, can be a little strange. One New Years, I performed at a restaurant that scheduled me in with another dancer. I wanted to see her show, so I changed into my second costume and as I quietly as I could I walked to a back wall so I could watch her, undetected by the audience. As she was dancing for one large table, she took her long hair which happened to be a black Repunzel wig, and flung the ponytail part at the table or I should say at one guy in particular. She whipped him in the face a few times before she sauntered off dancing for another table. I know my mouth was wide open and I tried not to laugh. The look on the man's face was total irritation and the reaction from everyone at the table was the same. The waiter came over to me and told me they were his table and that she was going to cost him a good tip.

The emotional roller coaster of dance has made me realize that part of entertaining people, isn't about presuming everyone will enjoy our interpretations of music. Becoming aware of our surroundings, means we are ambassadors, educating the masses in a way that is diplomatic. Dancing to our own tune means listening to the voice of present day opportunities as well as focusing on intentions that are enjoyable for everyone to experience. We can't follow our own tune, if we become deaf to what is happening around us. Following our own tune means we are considerate of the needs of those around us. I firmly believe our tune changes as we change, so you could be missing out in the most amazing time of your life, by simply tuning out what life is telling you. Life speaks to dancers specifically in music, and how we dance to her, says so much about how we hear her. If we aren't listening than we'll miss out on creative inspiration which is the life flow for all dancers. Ultimately, life speaks to us individually in ways that allows us to dance in our bliss.

Sometimes, I wonder if I am dancing my bliss or if I'm deluding myself. If I change my dance to fit how I live and view life, then am I a part of the changes happening in our dance form? Maybe this is the way our dance form survives, because we have to figure out various ways to fit her into modern day life. If following our tune keeps our dance form alive, then it seems obvious our dance form adapts naturally to change so that she can survive. The hard part is when you see changes happen, that you don't think are a part of your life choices. The ebb and flow of life seems to be linked to a variety of thought processes, that create a melting pot of ideas mixed together. All we can do is create and mold the type of dance we want, while we are in the moment. In the end, if we can do it in a way that keeps our part of the creative process truly our own inspiration, than it doesn't really matter what the changes are outside our path. It all merges together in a way that works.

Looking back on my path made me realize that most of my travels have been a solo journey. No one follows somebody else's tune, only because it isn't in our nature to follow what we can't hear. In a way, we have to trust in each other, as we are walking our path so that they parallel each other. This way it doesn't matter if we can't hear someone else's tune, we can still dance along side them because our sense of rhythm helps us fit in naturally with each other.

Listening to our tune is a unique way that the universe has of helping us develop our sense of who we are. When we stand up for what we believe in, we show the universe that we are listening and in the moment. So what happens when you have two paths that cross and they have nothing in common? We learn to be tolerant of each others opinions, even if they drive us insane. Life experiences are not always simple, and occasionally we do cross paths with people that in some form or fashion have something to teach us. The unfortunate part of learning like this is that the lesson is being given by someone you are not fond of or you don't trust. I don't like to be taught lessons this way but I have to admit, that the best lessons I have learned by far, are from people that I wasn't too fond of or who I am no longer friends with. Not all the lessons of life are learned at the same time, so we have to find those people who are similar in desires, aspirations and goals. Sometimes finding similarities in people is the lesson itself.

It's amazing how following our own tune is a lot like following our own intuition. I think they are one and the same, inspiring us to trust in ourselves and maybe gain trust in others.

As a wonderful quote from Alan Alda states," *You have to leave the city of your comfort and go into the wilderness of your intuition. What you'll discover will be wonderful. What you'll discover is yourself.*"

5 - Restaurant Dancing at it's Best & Worst

"Restaurant dancing brings out the Wonder Woman in Belly dancers. They encounter the unknown every time they dance between tables."

Restaurant dancing is such an art, not only because we dance in close proximity to customers, but because we have to understand people psychology. There have been evenings when I performed, where I was on cloud nine and then there were evenings where I wondered, what rock people crawled out from under. In certain restaurants, not only are we secondary to the food, but sometimes it feels like we compete with the customer's appetites, attitudes and phobias.

Restaurant Mortality

Throughout the years of dancing, I have been very blessed to have danced at some amazing restaurants, and then there were some that ended up becoming the antithesis called the twilight zone.

There were a few restaurants that I danced at that were open for only a few months. Those gigs are my most memorable, because I learned "what not to do" while dancing at a restaurant. If the restaurant owner requires you advertise at your own and expense and bring in family members, friends, co-workers and strangers off the street, you know you're in trouble. Imagine being asked to help out with washing the dishes. Oh yes, this did happen to me and at least I had enough sense to say "no" and suffice to say, that particular job lasted only a few weeks. Unfortunately for wait staff and entertainers, this is all too common a problem that we have to deal with. I loved the fact that at times, the wait staff and I followed the restaurant circuit together. It was almost like being apart of an underground community that was similar to being in the circus or vaudeville shows.

I remember one particular Persian restaurant that I danced at, wasn't doing well. One hot summer day in Dallas, I dressed up and walked the pavement, inviting businesses and people to come over to the restaurant and try the food. Little did I know, they were planning on closing the doors the following week. Imagine being in high heel shoes, walking on uneven sidewalks with pebbles or no sidewalks at all.

As I walked back through the restaurant door all sweaty and tired, I remember seeing a guilty look on the owners. He couldn't figure out how to tell me they were closing, especially since he knew I went and passed out flyers. I can't tell you how irritated I was with him for not telling me the truth. When I asked the owner why he didn't come clean with me, he started to complain about his circumstances, saying in a way we were all in the same boat. At that moment my feet totally disagreed! To this day there are parts of my feet that have never forgiven me. Big lesson learned, sometimes restaurants don't make it because the people running them don't have a clue.

Food for Thought

Some restaurants go through multiple owners and as a performer it can be interesting working around changes in protocol and personalities. I performed at one such restaurant-nightclub that went through two owners within a year and a half. The first owner was Egyptian and he created a nightclub-restaurant atmosphere that became popular quickly. I really liked dancing to the live band he brought in, and loved the nightclub atmosphere. The evenings were alive, full of people laughing and dancing. As time passed, I noticed the food started to go down hill, which eventually lead to empty tables and the regular crowd trickling away. I remember eating a soggy salad that had questionable tomatoes in it. Come to find out, it was made two days before and tasted like it. The owner was suspected of having a drug problem and it affected his ability to manage the restaurant.

New owners took over, who were from Turkey. They were a wonderful family who had a family table where everyone would gather around, talk and visit for hours. They brought in singers and musicians locally and abroad, that helped build up the clientele once more. The only problem with taking over a business like that is word of mouth. Even though the food improved, they had an uphill battle bringing in customers and packing them in on the weekends. I remember I had to walk across the kitchen barefoot in order to get to the main entrance which led to the dance floor. Sometimes the floor was sticky and gooey, so by the time I would get to the dance floor my feet would be black. I tried dancing in shoes and almost killed myself because so much of my training was barefoot. I bought shoes just to walk across the kitchen but the worst part was that sometimes the bottom of my skirt smelled like the kitchen floor. They closed down months later so the wait staff, musicians and I waited for another restaurant to open up because one always did.

People Psychology

Understanding people is so important in restaurant performing, because half the battle is seeing where people are coming from, or in other words their state of mind. It's necessary to do this first, so we can read people and their moods as soon as they walk through the front door. I have danced for people who didn't care if I could turn my head completely around, and spit out fire. They didn't come for my dancing, but for relaxation and food. I learned not to take this personally, and to go to tables more appreciative.

I noticed that if Americans don't have a particular interest in the culture we represent, misunderstandings happen that create problems. In many ways this can be a disadvantage for anyone, especially dancers themselves. Some American women unless they travel or educate themselves, see our dance form as a sexy dance done to provoke a reaction out of men and not just any man, theirs in particular. This is very obvious when attractive couples come in, because they put out a vibe that can be a little condescending. Here's a familiar scenario; the woman won't look at the dancer and her companion will stare at his plate, eating with enthusiastic gusto.

One experience I had was really funny. One Saturday, I was dancing at a restaurant in Albuquerque when a lady went up to one of the waiters and told him that her husband didn't like belly dancing. So the waiter, who was a good friend of mine, told me not to dance at their table. He was grinning when he told me because of one obvious fact, the tables were in an open room. I stayed away as requested, but I was visible, engaging the customers as I danced, from all angles in the room. As the evening progressed, I tried not to laugh, because as I was dancing for a table near the couple, her husband stood up and started to clap and dance along with me. It was obvious who really didn't want me to dance.

The Educated Priest

I have found that it's not only our job to educate the customers regarding our dance form, but it's also just as important to be lenient on their ignorance. It's not unusual for people to walk in the front door of a restaurant, and not know the first thing about belly dancing. For instance, I had a large party that requested, I not dance for them because they had invited a priest to join them. They were a church group that was concerned about the priests' reaction to my belly dancing. As I finished my show, I could hear the priest comment loudly that he enjoyed the show, what little he could see of it. I was surprised afterwards when he invited me to visit with him, so he could talk with me. He said he had been to the Middle East many times, and had seen belly dancing throughout his travels. He was very educated in our dance form and I really appreciated him letting the church group know, that he considered it an art form.

Apologizing for my Cane

Sometimes, even if people appreciate belly dancing, they don't always watch or pay attention. It's just the nature of the beast, when it comes to people getting together, and having a good time. On one particular evening, when I was dancing at a restaurant in Fort Worth, Texas, a group of women were enjoying themselves, talking loudly as I was performing my cane dance. I was a few tables away as I slowly danced my way towards them. As I finally approached their table, I unintentionally hit one of the ladies on the head with my cane as I twirled it. Thank God she had a hat on and a good sense of humor. After everyone at her table including me stopped laughing, I said, "That's what you get for not watching me." I then apologized profusely.

The Uncomfortable Hypocrite

I have noticed that some men don't know how to react to our dancing. It seems to stem from an uncomfortable reaction regarding their lack of knowledge concerning our dance form plus I think hidden issues. On one occasion, I was performing at a restaurant where it was obvious a male customer felt not only threatened, but hostile towards my dancing. He was trying to intimidate me, and for a short while I did feel slightly threatened not so much because he was a big man but because he absolutely wanted the dancing to stop. He was angry the duration of my performance, and when I went to a table close to his proximity, he stood up and physically, tried to stop me. The table I was dancing for booed him, and told me to keep on dancing. The owner came over immediately, telling him to calm down. Two other gentlemen stood up at the same time, just incase there was going to be trouble. I could sense this man's animosity which was a being instigated by his wife's bad attitude. He made a comment regarding lap dancing and the lack of family values, and the restaurant owner told him that since he knew so much about lap dancing then maybe he should take his family there. After more headed words were exchanged, the family got up to leave, and as they walked out the door, everybody in the restaurant applauded the owner, including me. That experience taught me a huge lesson; anyone can walk into a restaurant or nightclub not only with issues but a plate full of ignorance. These kinds of people have a false sense of what they think is appropriate and ethical.

Alcohol and Embarrassing Friends

Unfortunately, hypocrisy can include even our own friends who will eventually show their true colors with alcohol in their system. An ex-boyfriend had a business partner who joined us at a restaurant I danced at, with a companion. They were already drunk and obnoxious before they walked into the restaurant, disrupting other tables as they sat down. They were belligerent and rude to such a degree, that we had to ask them to leave. I apologized to the wait staff and the owner, making it clear they would never be allowed to come back. When my ex-boyfriend asked his business partner days later why she had acted so rudely, she said it was because she didn't like the culture. Needless to say, my relationship didn't last long because friends pretty much say a lot about who a person is. I didn't like what I was hearing and in the end, he ended up sounding just like his rude business partner.

Gypsy Kings

Probably the best restaurant experience I've ever had was when the Gypsy Kings were performing in Dallas, Texas. The weekend the Gypsy Kings were in concert, I just happened to be performing at a high end Italian restaurant in the downtown area. I was hired to perform for a large group of chiropractors, including their spouses. Unfortunately, I had to be at their beck and call the entire evening which meant performing, giving a lecture or a dance class at a moments notice. I entertained the wives for a couple of hours, so my saving grace was that I brought a variety of cds with me to dance to, which made time pass quickly. My favorite band was and is, the Gypsy Kings, so I incorporated their music into all my shows.

When everyone said their final good-byes, I was relieved because I was ready to unwind and eat dinner. Just as I was about to fall over in my chair from exhaustion, the bartender started to shout out that the Gypsy Kings were coming over to eat dinner. They had just finished performing a concert and they were in the mood for some good Italian food. The owner of the restaurant came over to my table, and asked me if I had it in me to do one more show. Not only did I come back to life, but I was jumping up and down ready to do summersaults. I just couldn't believe my good luck.

The minutes that passed by felt like an eternity, and I had to remember to breathe so I wouldn't pass out from the anticipation of waiting. With a yell from the valet drivers, we knew the Gypsy Kings had finally arrived. They pulled up in their limo and as the front doors opened, everybody in the restaurant started to clap. They came with an entourage that consisted of over twenty people, laughing and singing as they were directed to a long table. My moment of truth came, and I was introduced to everyone at the table. The whole group was gracious and very friendly but I have to say the Gypsy Kings were not only true gentlemen, but they seemed larger than life. They had an aura about them that was both magnetic and magical.

After about an hour, the owner signaled for me to get dressed. It was the first time in my life that I literally had butter fingers, because it seemed to take me twice as long to get ready. As I came out of the bathroom, I will never forget how amazing the feeling was to perform for the Gypsy Kings. I pinched myself just to make sure I wasn't dreaming. The bartender started to play my music and as they realized it was their own music, they laughed, clapped and sang along as I walked towards their table. In some ways, I felt like I was the one being entertained. I realized there are moments in life that take your breath away, and transport you to the divine. It was one big jam session, with everyone singing and dancing together! For me, this was a major career topper that even to this day, is my most memorable experience ever!

Pay Scale

The pay scale is a topic that is consistently a heated discussion amongst dancers. There's a reason for this, because one or two things happen to dancers who perform on a regular basis. The first problem is one I have talked about before, which is being undercut by other dancers. (I have been on both sides of the fence on this one, unintentionally). The second problem is working at a restaurant that is not willing to pay the going rate. In my 15 years of restaurant dancing, I found only a few restaurants that have paid me what I felt I was worth. I can count them on one hand. My philosophy is a little different here, only because I had to either come to terms with the reality of this business or get out.

One of my experiences with being undercut came about when I was dancing at a restaurant in Dallas. I had been performing for a few months as the only dancer at restaurant, so the restaurant owner hired two more dancers to perform on the weekends with me. I was relieved because I was getting tired of performing every weekend. What I didn't know, was their pay scale started at a higher rate then mine. One of the dancers had been performing for only a year, and it was obvious she wasn't hired for her dancing skills. After I found out, I talked to the owner and asked him why I was being paid less with more experience. He said he had just forgotten to give me a raise, so that night my pay went up. The owner just plain and simple was holding out because he was tightfisted with money.

In retrospect, I think the dancers felt it wasn't their place to tell me what they were being paid. They were a little embarrassed, but it was one of those situations where I had to correct it myself. In this business world, we are independent contractors so I think that each dancer has to speak up for her own self worth. In the end, I realized that worth is in the eye of the beholder and if we don't see our own worth, then how can we expect others to?

In a restaurant that I danced at in Albuquerque, the owner wanted to discuss each dancers pay individually because he felt it was a personal matter between him and each dancer. I agreed to a point, only because we had dancers coming in and out of the restaurant like a revolving door. I've worked at different restaurants where the dancers wanted to band together signifying a united front, in order to demand more money. It never worked, because there were always dancers willing to perform for less, waiting in the backdoor for the chance to take another dancers place. There are a lot of dancers who are waiting for their chance to dance, and when the pickings are slim for restaurants, the competition will do what it takes to get work like to work for a cheaper wage.

On the other hand, some dancers are hired for their figures and looks, not necessarily their talent or their lack of. Most dancer's in communities don't operate under a streamlined business protocol, unless they are apart of a studio or troupe. Some solo dancers don't base their business strategies for everybody else's benefit; they base their decisions on self motivated desires and an insatiable ambition to get to the top at all costs. The fact is, there will always be dancers around who just don't care about community ethics, especially if it means working together for the common good. Believe me, if I saw for one brief moment that we could unite and create a pay scale for all dancers, I would be the first one to join up. At my particular vantage point, I don't see it happening anytime soon. For dancers like me who are making a living with dancing, we have to make peace with the reality of what comes with this dance, which includes dancers who operate outside the etiquette modus operandi.

Making Lemonade out of Lemons

The restaurants that didn't pay me what I was worth were places for me to train and practice my dance and people skills. This is how I looked at them, period, with no regret or animosity. They were opportunities where I was able to perform on a regular basis, and work on my dancing in an environment that required me to do my best. So I feel you have to make the best out of every situation, and look on the positive side. Plus let's face it; no one forces us to perform at restaurants. If I'm dancing at a restaurant, I've made the decision and choice to be there. Remember, that the more experiences you have dancing in front of people, the greater your dancing skills will become for theater and night club performing.

Laugh

I retired from restaurant performing a few years ago, and looking back I have to laugh at some of the experiences I had. I can remember one evening, I was dancing and just happened to see my reflection in the window. At that very moment, I realized I forgot to shave my armpits. My arms went down immediately and I kept them down for the rest of my performance. After that, I always carried a razor in my makeup case. And believe it or not, I forgot my underwear a few times, so I put an extra pair in my bag for emergencies. One time I forgot my bra to my second costume, only to find it lying on my bed when I got home. I could have sworn, I put it in my bag. So I danced in the same costume twice, and as you can imagine it was sweaty! After that sweaty experience, I always had an emergency costume in my bag, just incase I forgot costume parts. A variety of things can happen at a moments notice, but they make the dancing experience that much more interesting and memorable.

The one bit of advice I would give to any dancer starting out performing in restaurants, is the venue itself will help any dancer become a better performer. I feel restaurant dancing made a big difference in my nightclub and stage performing, because it made me a more personable dancer. Belly dancing encompasses so many things, one being the desire to entertain audiences far and wide. Restaurant dancing allows for each dancer to perform with a personal grace that is backed by confidence and people skills. This is invaluable because most women who perform in restaurants can dance just about anywhere. Plus, one day you will look back at your restaurant years, and like me have great memories to share with family and friends. It's in the sharing itself that makes restaurant memories, truly "priceless".

6 - Stage Fright

"Stage Fright has the timing of a punctual nemesis that reminds us we are mortal just seconds before we prepare to go on stage."

Can you remember the first time you ever saw belly dancing? With my six year old eyes, I knew this dance was where I wanted to be. Funny how we envision grandeur and fame, yet it never enters our mind that each aspiration or goal has to be experienced within its own time. The stage was like a beckoning jewel; she called to me and whispered in my ear that I was meant to be performing on her. I wasn't quite sure exactly what this meant but with gusto, I leaped onto my first stage like a gazelle, only to land flat on my face. The deer caught in the headlights look took on a whole new meaning, because I became its poster child.

My dance debut was a combined effort with the New Mexico Dance Coalition and New Directions Gallery on the Taos plaza. My first instructor Dina, was one of the top ten choreographers touring through out New Mexico for that summer. Because the New Mexico Dance Coalition was passing through Taos, Dina felt it would be a wonderful opportunity for me to debut my choreography to the local residents. At this point, I had just come back to Taos after working cattle in Mexico and Texas during the winter months, so I had to switch from cowgirl to belly dancer as soon as I got back. I must admit, Dina had to twist my arm and do some finger pointing finagling, before I would say yes. With the word yes coming out of my mouth, I realized my dream of performing in front of my Taos community, was finally coming true. So I worked on my choreography and forged ahead for months in preparation of my debut. As the date of the performance was coming closer and closer, I found that a slight panic would set in and I would have to convince myself that all I had to do was survive the performance. I was actually looking at my calendar and wishing that the performance date had already passed, and I was reminiscing to friends about the show: Little did I know that this was my first experience with stage fright.

The rehearsal day came rolling around and I had butterflies in my stomach all day. I had no idea the show was going to be televised and it was probably a good thing because I would have either fainted or hyperventilated if I had known. I thought the unthinkable might happen and it did. When it was my turn to step onto to the dance floor during rehearsal, I went numb and my brain froze. The camera guy was right in front of the stage, waiting for me to begin along with all the people who were working behind the scenes. I did a total melt down right in front of everybody, and all I could do was spin. I was crying as I left the stage, amongst the chuckles of everyone watching. The camera guy just shook his head, and I'm sure he was thinking I was going to totally bomb that evening. He wasn't the only one, I had my doubts too. Dina grabbed me at the end of rehearsal, and told me to work out my choreography on the dance floor, and to pretend like no one was watching me. So I went back out and did as she suggested. As I did this, my choreography came back to me, and I actually received applause from the remaining backstage crew at the end of my performance. I felt better but my eyes were swollen from crying and my self confidence was slightly bruised.

Hours later, as I was standing behind the dancer in front of me, who was being announced, my bladder all of a sudden couldn't hold a drop of water, and my stomach churned and gurgled loudly. My palms were sweaty and I knew my pupils were dilated. I was reprimanding myself for saying, yes and it was all I could do not to run. I thought, if I ran out the back door, nobody would notice. As all of this was going through my mind, a thunderous applause erupted from the stage area, and the backstage manager said, "You're up." As the dancer entered the back room out of breath and glowing from her performance, she whispered, "Break a leg." All I knew at that moment was that my heart was in my throat and it stayed there. As my name was announced, I walked onto the stage terrified and gasping for air. I felt like all the air inside me had been squeezed out of me by an invisible corset. Thank God my music started, because as I heard the first phrasing in the music, I noticed that I was actually starting to enjoy myself and breath. The end of my music came in what seemed like a blink of an eye and before I knew it, I was in front of a standing room only audience, bowing to a deafening applause. Backstage Dina was crying, and told me I danced beautifully and how proud she was that I went through with it. I on the other hand just wanted to collapse on the floor, and relish in the fact that I had survived my first experience with stage fright.

Stage Fright Characteristics are interesting to experience and as we survive them, we get a better grasp of our own phobias and fears. Here, I put together some characteristics, in a way that I think will help the inner dancer in you laugh at herself. I truly believe that laughter is the best medicine for stage fright and every time I think of my performance in Taos, I laugh and smile. It's one of my fondest memories because I learned that I had it in me to be a dancer that night, and from that day forward, I never looked back.

#1 Sneaky and Clever

First and foremost, stage fright is very clever. It sneaks up on dancers just before they get ready to perform, instigating an argument between their mortality and dance persona. All the passion that dancers feel over the weeks of preparation is inundated with trivial insecurities that try their damndest to create havoc for those few brief moments before a performance. Their timing is impeccable.

#2 Sleep Paralyses

It is amazing how stage fright affects the body. You may wake up on the morning of your performance, feeling like you shouldn't get out of bed. You take delight in hiding under the covers, thinking you might stay there all day. A tired feeling slowly overwhelms the body, making nap time very appealing. This feeling always happened just before I was about to drive to a restaurant or nightclub. There would be a ten minute period, where I would feel like I was driving with one eye open and one eye closed.

#3 Bladder Issues

My bladder habitually transformed itself into the size of a pea, just before my performances. I remember one incident at a club in Dallas, I was performing with a band called the Arabic Band and saw stars literally. During my performance, I felt like I was going to pass out from dehydration. Since I didn't want to have to go to the bathroom five times before I was scheduled to perform, I decided not to drink any water. On this particular night, the club was packed full of people and the spot lights seemed hotter then usual. Unbeknownst to me, the drummer was in an exhilarated mood, so my drum solo was a long one. I was soaking wet, from perspiring and my lips were parched and dry. By the end of my show, I felt dizzy and exhausted. I ran to the back dressing room, only to collapse on the floor. It took three bottles of water before I was cooled down and hydrated. Lesson learned, I would rather go to the bathroom five times instead of passing out on a dirty floor.

#4 Heart to Heart

For some reason, just before a performance my heart would beat all over the place and never stay where it belonged. It would either, try to jump out of my throat or head south for my knees. There were a few times, I thought it was gone because I literally couldn't feel it anywhere. I could only assume it fell out somewhere and hopefully would find it's way back. But I must say, even with all these feelings, the one thing the heart does for us, is it keeps us real and in the moment. Within these precious moments, the heart is pumping, jumping and skipping us through our performance. It keeps the memory alive, because emotion is the best way to remember a performance.

#5 Pimples and Break outs

The occasional break out is one of the worst of stage frights characteristics, because it's an unnecessary evil. I think there is a *Pimple Pixie* that exists for this very reason. I can remember I was dancing for an anniversary party at a restaurant I use to perform at. I woke up the morning of the performance with this huge bump in the middle of my forehead. It wasn't there the day before and I took extra measures to make sure my skin was clear. As you might have guessed, stage fright had something to do with it. So what did I do...all I can say is "Thank God for bindis!" With the *Pimple Pixie* in cahoots with stage fright, not only are they an indomitable team but sneaky too!

#6 Hallucinations

Example: Curtains

The brain for all its virtues is susceptible to stage fright overloading it with images that aren't really there or are they? Stage curtains can be the best example of this. In a major production that I co-produced in 2008, a very funny incident happened to me that must have looked ridiculous from the side of the stage. I was wearing a mask for my performance, and with the lights blinding me from all directions; I couldn't see where the curtains were compared to the walk space. I was dressed as a warrior type of character in our play that had just slain a dragon and its minions. So as the lights blacked out at the end of my performance, I started to walk to the side of the stage which was pitch-black. I unfortunately walked right into the curtains and tangled myself up, in one of them. A few of the dancers watching from the sidelines took pity on me, untangled me and guided me to the side door. As they escorted me towards the right direction, a few giggles could be heard in the silence. I would have laughed myself but at that moment, I was part blind and a bit humiliated. For some odd reason I just knew those curtains were going to get the best of me and they did.

Stage Morphing

The stage can either become larger or smaller depending on what false image stage fright creates in your brain. I have been on a stage that when I walked on it, I was fine and it was the perfect size, but as the moment came for me to perform on it, I felt like it was swallowing me up and I was going down a rabbit hole. It seemed so small, that I felt like I was going to fall off at any moment! Furthering the rabbit-hole phenomenon, I almost spun off a stage into the audience, because it felt like I teetered to one side. It didn't matter how I positioned myself on this particular stage, because any turns or spins I did came close to becoming wipe outs. The worst part was that the stage was up high, so if I would have wiped out, I would have been a contender for funniest home videos and the end of my career.

Unfriendly Audience

This next false image can really work on a dancer's self image because it materializes the unfriendly audience. I have left the stage thinking that the audience didn't like me, only to find out afterwards that I was well received. I have come to the conclusion that my brain has a lot of empty compartments in it that can be filled at a moment's notice, with false images without me even knowing it. The problem is, we usually don't know where these compartments are, so they can fill up at any minute. If I knew where these compartments were, I'd bar the doors shut.

#7 Music Malfunctions

I'll never forget a performance I saw years ago, where a dancer came onto the stage late. She could never catch up to her music, and her finger cymbal playing was off from the beginning. They emphasized how behind she was, and it was uncomfortable to listen to and watch. It was a wonderful lesson to learn, because music doesn't know it has to catch up or slow down for a dancer.

Music bloopers have happened to me in restaurants, especially with customers chatting and talking; it can be an unintentional mess up with the noise factor. One time my performance cd somehow became scratched and it kept repeating itself, so my finger cymbals couldn't be played at all. The skipping made them constantly behind or ahead to the point that I had to laugh. Playing finger cymbals with another dancer can also get your timing off. If the patterns aren't the same, finger cymbals can become an unintentional cacophony that can be hard on the ears.

#8 CD Problems

I have been blessed to be a featured performer in a few workshop shows in Roswell, by invitation from my friends Alice and Mathew. In one particular show, I had a major music malfunction that couldn't be fixed. For some reason my cd worked perfectly during rehearsal but it wouldn't play at all for my performance. Mathew played the cd over and over and tried to fix the problem but to no avail. I had another cd with me, and thought it would be fun to let the audience pick the music they wanted me to dance to. So I asked the audience if they would like to do this and they applauded enthusiastically with a yes. I ended up dancing to various songs of the audiences choosing, and showed my students that performing has a lot to do with the comfort level a dancer has within her own dance persona. I also showed them that the show must go on, and as a professional dancer you roll with the punches.

#9 Prop Malfunctions

There is always this feeling in the back of my mind, that stage fright in some way is responsible for various props acting up during my performances. I think malfunctions are a form of stage fright in a way, because when anything unpredictable happens during a performance, it can deflate the enthusiasm out of any dancer. The veil is a good example of this, because there is nothing like working with a veil that acts up. As most of us have found out, it doesn't discriminate between a novice or experienced dancer, we are all fair game.

Even with a dancer's energetic grace, I found out tables can become a hazard. One time, when I was dancing at a restaurant I twirled in front of a couple, and knocked over their wine bottle, only to grab it on a spin before it hit the ground. They were laughing with amazement and delight at my display of agility. I, on the other hand, just about panicked and had to swallow my heart.

I'll never forget another instance where I showered people with my veil because I twirled into a water fountain. Some people thought it was funny while others glared at me. My veil was soaking wet which made me look like I had been playing in the fountain. The restaurant owner just laughed, and told me to do my veil dancing in the other rooms instead.

The Moment Stage Fright Slips Away

The first time I felt at ease on stage, was during a workshop show where the pandemonium was intense. I was in line ready to go on after a dancer who was supposed to be in front of me, but unfortunately she was no where to be found. So the backstage manager told me I was up next, instead of the other dancer. Just as I was about to be announced, the other dancer rushed up behind me, frantically trying to catch her breath. So the backstage manager told me to step aside, so she could perform on her scheduled time. As I stepped aside, the sound supervisor said he couldn't find her music, and that mine was ready to go. I was told to get back inline again, so they would have time to find the other dancer's music. As all this was happening I remember, I couldn't wait to get on stage, and as my music began, it was as if time stood still and all that existed was the audience, the music and my dance. It's a milestone that I will always remember, because stage fright was nowhere in site!

Tips

With stage fright always lurking around, I thought it would be fun to share some tips my friends and I came up with to help overcome such a calculating adversary:

1. Laugh with friends and think of whatever makes you happy - There is no failure in performing, because if you don't go out on stage, you will never know what it feels like to be in front of an audience. People appreciate heart felt efforts!

2. Have family and friends in the front row to cheer you on. My daughter makes me smile because she is my greatest supporter.

3. Know your music like the back of your hand. Even if you forget your choreography the music will be very familiar to you.

4. Go over your choreography the morning of your performance and try to keep it fresh in your mind. I will usually listen to my music on the drive to wherever I am performing. It helps jazz me up and sometimes I'll come up with some interesting moves in my head. (Be careful of the belly dancer pedal to the metal groove!)

5. Remember to practice your performance with your costume on. I have danced with a skirt that could fit a whole circus in it.

6. Remember to look in the mirror just before you go on stage, and smile at the beautiful dancer looking back at you. (Plus it doesn't hurt to check to see if lipstick is on your teeth!)

7. The stage is really our friend. Know the length and width of any space you are performing on. There's nothing you can do with hallucinations, so feel comforted by facts not phobias.

8. When dancers perform together they become apart of an amazing team so know you have support and back up on the side lines. You are not alone!!

9. A good meditation or prayer will always put a heart or soul at ease. Group prayer can really give you the boost you need and send stage fright running!

10. This next bit of advice is from my friend Rozana; remember to stretch, relax and breathe. Focusing on your breathing will help with jitters and apprehension.

11. Last but not least is stage frights final illusion, which is the expectation of standing ovations and a movie deal your first time performing. Granted not all of you may have fallen for this one, but I sure did. As the saying goes, ignorance is bliss that is until you find out you're in a long line of hopefuls just like yourself.

Sometimes it doesn't matter how long a dancer has been performing, those apprehensive feelings can stay in the background up until the very moment just before the curtain opens. It's as if stage fright has a way of creeping in every once in awhile, just to say hello. I experienced this when I went back to Dallas, to perform at a nightclub a couple of years ago. I had performed there years earlier and loved it. I was invited back as a guest dancer, and I felt like expectations were raised slightly, since I had just put out my first instructional video "Hip Phylosophy". Just before I was announced and ready to come out on the stage, I noticed my palms were sweaty and that I couldn't catch my breath. The atmosphere in the nightclub was starting to come back to me. The energy was alive and I loved being back, because I missed the lively atmosphere that had at one time been a part of my life. As I stepped forward onto the stage, I felt like I was home again.

Stage fright is really about being alive and aware in the moment. It can be a blessing in disguise, because as a performer we have to feel every fiber of our being. And when I'm in my rocking chair years from now thinking of my dance career, I don't want to just remember it, I want to relive it in my memories and know that I lived dance to its fullest.

7 - Belly Dance Bloopers

"If dancing were any easier it would be called football."

Anonymous

What can I say? If it could happen, it did happen to me! Just about every dancer out there has a blooper story to tell. Bloopers are almost like a right of passage and there are a lot of us out there that are seasoned veterans of the occasional blooper.

Bloopers can happen for many reasons, for example, skipping the essential costume checklist, to make sure your snaps and hooks are sewn on tightly. Let's be honest here, when you dance every weekend and perform 2 to 4 shows a night, your costumes will start to suffer. I had multiple costumes that I regularly checked for any malfunctions before I packed for the night and selected what I would wear. As time passed, my costume check regimen jumped out the window. By appearance, my costumes looked good but hidden from the general public, were pins here and there holding together a strap or skirt. From seemingly minor malfunctions, my bloopers came to life leaving me with their embarrassing memories.

Snaps and Hooks

I remember, I was dancing for a recreational camp for kids, where there had to be at least 200 kids ranging in ages from kindergarten up to teenagers. They were all watching me perform in a large rec. room. Before I knew it, as I was doing one of my favorite turns, the hook holding together my back strap broke and there for a few seconds were my breasts bared for everyone to see. The younger kids didn't quite get what had happened, but the older ones did. Fortunately I had my niece, Sarah with me who pinned my back straps together (laughing hysterically, I might add) so I could continue my performance. To my dismay, the group leaders were already guiding the kids out of the room, and only a few stayed to see me finish. I don't think I helped our community out much with that performance. To my knowledge they haven't invited any belly dancers back. Moral of the story: Check your snaps and hooks!

Bra Pads

Weight fluctuation, is another blooper waiting to happen. I learned the hard way, that my daughter's socks are not a good substitution for bra pads. I had lost weight and fixed a few costumes, but not all of them. The quick fix was my daughter's socks. They gave me the boost I needed, and I figured no one would know the better of it. I wore two of my favorite costumes for a huge dinner party of VIPs at Pars Cuisine in Albuquerque, New Mexico. One came with sewn in bra pads, the other came with socks. Unfortunately, because I was lazy, the obvious disaster was just waiting to happen…and it did. Have you ever had that impending, gut feeling that something isn't right, well I had it, but I actually wasn't worried because I had used my daughter's socks before with no problem, but socks as I found out have a mind of their own.

The dinner party was for a large group of diplomats, who were a great audience, congenial and ready to be entertained. Everybody was yelling my name and clapping as I came out ready to dance the night away. And that was exactly what I was doing until I noticed a few grins and giggles from the audience, which for your information was almost all men. One man pointed to my bra and from my vantage point, my breasts and bra looked fine. But when I did a chest circle, there to my horror was my daughter's sock hanging down my right side. So I did what any professional belly dancer would do (not really), I pulled it out and threw it towards the wait staff. Everybody laughed and applauded as I continued to dance, but unfortunately there was nothing I could do with my pushed up breast and the significantly smaller one. After the evening was over and everybody had left, I went looking for my daughter's sock. I couldn't find it anywhere and even had the wait staff (who were still giggling) help me look for it. But it was no where to be found. Weeks passed and I forgot about the missing sock, until the owner of the restaurant told me that my sock was given to the head diplomat as a gift and memento of his visit. So whoever took it, had it framed and presented it to him. Also to go along with the sock, were 5 video cameras that captured the infamous sock rolling incident.

So moral of this story: bra pads!

Skirts and Tables

Long skirts, can be a bloopers best friend. I like my skirts long because I am short, and if my skirts are just a little above my ankles, they make me look even shorter. So the bottom of my skirts, get really dirty and I have to wash them a lot. I had one particularly long skirt that I just loved. It was separate from my belt, and I loved this because I could mix and match to my hearts content. One evening, I wore this skirt with my costume for a big dinner party at a nightclub I use to dance at. The family who had the dinner party, had specifically asked for me, so I was very honored to dance for them. The night began very innocently, with me dancing around tables and on chairs. They even put me up on the tables a few times. It's amazing what your skirt can get caught on, and tables have no mercy for the unsuspecting dancer. I was dancing to my favorite drum solo song while I was on a table, when I decided to end my performance on stage. So I jumped down off the table, and began to stroll over to the stage only to realize that my skirt didn't want to come with me. As a few customers tried to get me unstuck, my skirt somehow got pulled down and was close to my knees. Finally, my skirt was pulled free and I gracefully pulled my skirt up and was able to finish the last minute of my show. The family loved the little drama, and said they would remember that night for a long time. The moral of this story: Wear matching underwear and don't dance on tables!

Props

Props can either be a friend or foe. Sometimes I really believe my veil, cane or sword took sides with the bloopers. You know how it is, you practice in the studio or home and everything goes great, but as soon as you get out the door and go perform some place, something bizarre happens to your prop. I have often wondered if my props were possessed. It's amazing how your veil will get caught on your costume or how your cane flies out of your hand. My sword was better behaved but would occasionally act up too.

One evening in Fort Worth, I was dancing in a very crowded restaurant performing with my cane. Everybody was enjoying themselves and the owner of the restaurant was sitting at a table not far from our little stage. I was twirling the heck out of my cane, when to my surprise the cane flew out of my hand and landed on top of the restaurant owners lap. The whole restaurant applauded and yelled for more. I slowly went up to the restaurant owner and asked for my cane back and as he handed it to me, he had an amused look on his face. Fortunately for me, my cane music was almost over so I didn't have to try for an encore. So the moral of this story; if you mess up with your prop, make it look good!

Wrong Party

Sometimes arriving at a performance space can be very confusing, especially if there are wall to wall people talking, yelling and laughing. It's amazing what can happen at unfamiliar nightclubs. The feeling is similar to Alice going down the rabbit hole.

Years ago, I was hired by a couple to perform at a club in the Albuquerque downtown area. I was excited for two reasons, I had just raised my prices and the couple who hired me didn't blink an eye at my price, and they paid me in advance with the promise of great tips. Looking back, I'm so grateful that I followed my instincts and came dressed to the club because the bathrooms were constantly crowded with women streaming in. The only other room available was a back room where the club stored their liquor. The bartender didn't seem to mind sharing, especially since there was no lock on the door, so I politely declined.

As I looked around for the contact person who I had never met, I was bombarded with people wanting me to dance with them. So I danced a little as I crossed the crowded room, with people laughing and clapping. I was at the club for about an hour and to my dismay, no contact person approached me. I called them, getting no answer so I decided to wait, since I knew they would eventually find me. I was standing by a table, when a man approached me and started to talk to me. I couldn't hear him because the music was so loud, but the part that was slightly audible did lead me to believe he was the contact person. I told him I was ready to dance and with a nod he started to guide me to where his party was. Through the throngs of people, he waved his hand and directed me to follow him to an upstairs room. He gave my music to a DJ, and I started my show which ended up being a twenty minute performance, and then the next half hour was dancing with everybody, and teaching them a few moves here and there.

At the end of the hour, I was wet with perspiration and excused myself to go and cool down. I went into the women's bathroom to dry myself off, when a woman approached me and asked if I was Leyla Najma. I told her yes I was, and she said that her group had been waiting for me for almost two hours. My mouth dropped open and I just stared at her, with the dumbest look on my face. I told her I had tried to call them and she said that she had been trying to call me too. At this point, I told her I was dancing for a group I had assumed was her party. She laughed (thank God) and said who ever they were, they weren't her apart. I started to laugh, because I told her a man approached me, who I thought was her husband who led me to a party upstairs. Needless to say, the upstairs group got a free show from me besides free dance classes.

My journey that night made a major zigzag, but I eventually ended up dancing for the right party. I stayed an extra hour as an apology for the unfortunate delay. But I must admit, I had such a good time, minutes turned into hours and hours turned into an evening where time didn't exist. To this day, I really don't know who that man was, but all I know is after that fiasco, I made sure there was always a designated meeting place. Moral of the story; If you dance for the wrong party, at least make sure they know how to tip!

The Hidden

The hidden bloopers are the ones that can really make any dancer feel like she is walking into the unknown. You know what I'm talking about; hidden bloopers only reveal themselves at the very moment a dancer can't do much about it. For instance, there you are on stage dancing and than you realize that the stage is uneven or worse, you just stepped on something that feels very slimy and gooey. Most of the time, I don't even look down if I step on something gross because if I do, I know it will affect my performance and not in a good way.

The Shrinking and Uneven Stage

The shrinking stage seems to have a connection with Houdini. It's not always possible when we get hired to dance to check the stage out before hand. I remember when I was hired for a party, I asked how big the space was and the family replied that it was a good sized space, at least half of a room. So I choreographed accordingly to what I was told. Half a room ended up being a space that was 4ft by 4ft. The worst part was they had me in front of a raging fireplace due to the fact it was winter. With little kids sitting all around me, my choreography which included spinning with a sword changed immediately, and I was amazed that I didn't pass out from the heat.

The uneven stage is the one blooper that hides itself very well. I have been on stages that looked level but when I danced on them they turned me into a lopsided sideshow. At one particular restaurant, whenever I would spin, I would slowly but surely spin into a table on the right side of the stage, stopping just short of losing it. I finally asked the other dancers if they did the same thing and they all replied yes. What a relief, because I didn't want to be the only lopsided dancer.

Unintentional Splits

Anytime I think of my slimy stories they give me the creeps because just imagining what could be imbedded between my toes grosses me out. If you dance at restaurants, unfortunately goopy and greasy left overs are a reality. The worst realization is when a dancer can feel herself slipping or sliding on an unknown object, only to find out with a quick glance that it's a chicken leg! That's right; I was one of those dancers that did the unintentional splits because of a chicken leg that was dropped on the floor by an unknown 3 year old.

I happen to be dancing for a large group which included numerous kids, who occasionally lost their food or dropped it on the floor…out of excitement from my dancing. Okay, maybe I'm pushing it a little, but I'll never forget the moment when I was spinning with my cane on my head, when I felt something stuck between my toes. Not only was I in pain, but at first I wasn't sure what it was. All kinds of gross and creepy images came into my mind within seconds. Since I was on the ground in agony, I looked to see what the culprit was that had done me in, and there between my toes was a half eaten chicken leg. I had to literally pull it out between my toes and then deal with the grease from the floor that got all over my skirt. I could feel the unintentional splits for weeks afterwards, and considered wearing shoes thereafter. Moral of the story; No matter how cute the kids are they have it in them to do the belly dancer in.

Chairs

The straw that broke the camels back in regards to shoes happened because of a chair. I was dancing for a large birthday party with my sword on my head, when I spun a little too close to a chair. I was half way through my show and I could tell something was wrong with my baby toe on my right foot. I couldn't feel it. I was pulled up on a chair shortly afterwards and to keep my balance, I was placing my weight on my toes and again I couldn't feel my baby toe on my right foot. I finished my show and went back into the dressing room so I could look down and check out my toe. A panic feeling sunk in, when I saw my baby toe bent out to the right side like a thumb. I just looked at it for a few minutes before I was started to lose it. I yelled, and the owner came into the dressing room to see what the matter was. I showed him my toe, and he immediately told me I would have to go to the hospital. Lady luck was with me, because there happened to be an older gentleman who was from Korea eating dinner that night. He was sitting at a table nearby, when he motioned for me to come over to the table and sit down. As I sat down crying, he took my foot into his lap to take a look at my toe. He made a funny noise that made me laugh, and that's when he pushed my toe back into place. It didn't even hurt when he did it. I was shocked and relieved and cried a little more because I felt like such a baby. I found out the gentleman was a martial arts master, so he was used to dealing dislocated toes. The next day, I had a bruise up the side of my foot almost to my knee. After that experience, I wore my first pair of dance shoes ever!

So these are just a few of my blooper stories. The one thing I realized throughout my 25 years of performing is even though I strive for perfection in my dance, the bloopers keep me grounded. They make me think back and laugh at the dumb and embarrassing things that have happened to me. If you laugh at yourself then you have just given yourself a wonderful gift. Laughter keeps us humble and it keeps us healthy.

8 - Life is a Stage

"A dancer on stage performing just for the pure joy of it is more then an accomplished dancer, she is a woman content with herself."

Lights, camera, and oh yeah...for a minute I forgot where I was. Isn't it amazing what a stage can do to you? For most dancers including myself, we have had the pleasure and displeasure of dancing on a variety of dance floors, some of which seem to be in the oddest of places and surroundings. There are times when it feels like tons of people are sucking the air out of us, making us feel as if we're gasping for our last breath. Outside venues, can bring unimaginable problems that leave lasting impressions. Black tar covered spaces in the hot sun, or pebbles and small rocks, frequently become our feet and toes worst nightmare. Let's not forget dancing in spaces with intoxicated people, some in high heels who couldn't dance even if they were sober. My toes would scream in horror, every time a drunken customer danced within a few feet of me.

Come to think of it, I guess I have danced on just about every type of dance floor imaginable. I've danced on grass, which is fine for the most part, except for the occasional hidden, gopher sized hole. Tables are very interesting, giving you height, but I don't recommend them, especially if they wobble or you get stuck with enthusiastic fans that won't let you down. I have found chairs to be my enemy and definitely don't recommend them. Brick patios with little pebbles are a major problem for any dancer who does floor work or spins. Carpet is great, except for the occasional carpet burn either on the bottom of your feet or knees. Probably, my least favorite space to dance on is the sloping hill, because there is no saving grace if you roll down or twirl off into another yard. Once a dancer finds herself on a "real" stage, she has the sense of making it, because when the lights are upon us and the curtains lift, it's all about the dance, isn't it?

Living life from one stage to the next creates a different type of mindset that most people don't understand. As dancers, we approach everything in life with an avant-garde and intrinsic belief system because we walk paths least traveled by the main stream populace. There is a certain satisfaction knowing that we are not only different, but with an eccentrically animated point of view. I believe this is why we are needed because we are the refuge that viewers seek, so they can escape from their everyday reality. Audiences have the choice to participate in our world at their leisure, unfortunately if we don't watch our own point of reference, we can get lost in the maze of our own design. The stage can lose its appeal as a refuge even for dancers. Sometimes the only validation dancers will accept in regards to who they are as women, is the stage. It can entrap even the truest of hearts because the draw for most women is to be recognized for their ability to express their own creativity. In the end, it's really about being liked for individual creative expression.

Validation is important for dancers but it can create a distorted view of the stage, almost like a hall of mirrors that makes everyone disoriented. The stage can become more important than the audience, with dancers drowning in the meaning of their dance. I think the question that we must ask ourselves, is what is it that we want people to see and remember when they see us dance on stage? The irony for most dancers is that the everyday grind for them, is entertaining the masses. Just like every dancer has to figure out what their refuge is, they also have to maintain their original purpose for entertaining. It's easy at times to forget the naivety and excitement of beginning passions. Sometimes I found that my costumes at various points in my career became my work clothes.

Giving ourselves to the audience night after night can become an addiction. The audience's applause can become an adrenalin rush like a daily fix. There has to be a give and take that balances itself out because our needs have to be replenished, by stepping back and seeing the forest for the trees. As in life a stage can become something you never expected. The lessons learned can leave the remains of emotional baggage that can be utilized on stage. The trick is to dance out the lessons in a way that replenishes the soul instead of depleting it.

I can remember performing at a night club with a friend of mine. She had complained about dancing with another performer, who previously hogged the spotlight the whole time they were performing together. The funny thing is that evening my friend did the exact same thing to me. She was planted on the middle of the dance floor, right on the point where the spotlight was shining. So I danced in front of her towards the audience and played up on the close proximity of the tables. The audience started to laugh because it became obvious what I was doing. I had to improvise the best I could and for a few brief moments I felt like I was dancing a déjà Vu rendition of my dance friend's experience.

This is what makes dance so enticing, because life doesn't always tell us what's around the corner or where we'll end up after we spin. Do we become wonder women as performers and average women by day? I have often wondered what happens to dancers when they believe too much in their dance persona. I have seen dancers forget that they are mortal especially living the belly dancer's life. It's as if the stage seduces the senses, and after a while of embracing the intoxicating allure of lights, sound and applause, dancers change into their own nemesis, creating the very adversary within themselves they abhor.

Is the stage our friend, sometimes I wonder because I have witnessed men and women lose their humility at the first sight of a stage. It's almost as if the only way a dancer can prove their worth even to themselves, is on a stage. I wonder why we feel we have to prove anything at all. Isn't living life enough? For the entertainer the answer is not so easily defined because we seek validation in everything we do. Entertainers always seem to push the envelope, because we want to see what's over the next horizon. Dancers are constantly looking for the latest new move or inspiration. Our downfall can be that we are blinded to what

53

is closest to home. How we express ourselves outside of dance is just as important, probably more so then when we are on stage. We have to remember, the stage is not only an escape from reality but a way that all of us can express the reality in which we live. Obviously the stage doesn't always work out like we hope but this only parallels life because sometimes life doesn't either.

In truth, the stage seems to be a vessel in which we are able to work out our issues that we hold onto or carry within our bodies. As I look back at various stages I have performed on, I can see they represented freedom from the constraints that I allowed to rule my life. We can show the world we are not definable at least by their standards. For timeless moments on a stage, we can show the world how it feels and looks to be in the moment, defined only by surrendering to our dance.

The stage has allowed me to be experience personalities, and they have all been very healing because trying on all the different facades of life can be eye opening. I can be anyone on stage, accepted by the audience and do all this without anyone ever knowing that I am dancing with assorted faces of my phobias, fears and issues. In many ways as dancers, we are blessed because the stage is the sacred ground for healing and restoring hope in us all. The stage is the immediate connection from the dancer to the divine, that is witnessed by the audience in an avant-garde way. It's human nature to become transfixed with something so personal yet so open and shared freely.

Maybe life is really one, gigantic stage and everywhere we go, we perform our lives. In the end, it doesn't matter where the stage is, because if we are in our living rooms or performing in a night club, we share who we are with those around us. Each day, life gives us a new script, and turning the pages is the best part. If we didn't make the pages come to life then we wouldn't have anything to dance for. It's apparent that the stage represents so much for so many dancers, because they reveal parts of their lives to the masses. Maybe this will sound cliché, but it seems to me that the stage is really a sacred space where we grow, learn, step back from life and escape into; it's the eternal circle of life.

When I speak of surrendering to my definition of my dance, I am speaking from a different place that only dancers understand. I have found dancing for my peers can be more stressful than the general populace, but in some immeasurable way they seem to understand my efforts. As dancers, we know that performing is our way of life, so we create a bond with each other every time we dance. Again this is where the stage comes in and is an integral part of our way of communicating with each other. Sometimes we are introduced after we see each other perform on stage. This is what is so amazing about dance; the first glance of creative efforts is our hello to each other. So the stage in a symbolic way, introduces us to each other. If for no other reason, this sets us apart from the main stream populace, because whether we like or dislike a performance, there is always an understanding of the creative process that frees us. As a community, we walk amongst each other knowing that in a sense we are freer then the average woman because we are able to create our own works of art, continually through out our dance lives. When I look at a stage, I don't just see freedom and a connection with other dancers, I see home. As Dorothy in the Wizard of Oz said, "There's no place like home," dancers say, "There's no place like the stage."

9 - Weighing in on My Belly Dance Image

"Belly Dance is a fatal attraction for women that entice them into their labyrinth with the impassioned need to be skilled in her art."

Sometimes when I look in the mirror, there standing before me is a blurred impression of me. Now that I am in my forties, losing weight is a different journey that is intimidating and daunting. I don't necessarily look at my image and see only what I don't like because every once in awhile I'll surprise myself and see my Mae West impersonation rockin it. Occasionally, all I want to do is envision plastic surgery alternatives, so a war rages in me for a few days until I make peace with myself.

This is not only contradictory to what I tell my students, but I have become the human icon for this paradox. I usually tell them to look in the mirror and see what they like about themselves, but sometimes even for myself, there's a grey area. I guess I'm telling my students so I can remind myself, to keep looking for the undiscovered diamond in the rough. I wonder if it's normal with age, to constantly try to convince oneself that everything is as good as it used to be, almost new. Lately, I have been coming to terms with the fact that I wake up a little slower in the morning then I use to. I talk to my body and tell her how lucky we are because we have a career where dance is an everyday occurrence. But I have to admit that my body doesn't always want to listen to me.

Body image, visualization is important for all women, especially for dancers. Unfortunately, we can be judged harsher then the average woman and with today's standards, it can get a bit ridiculous. A while back, I read statistics that stated the ideal woman is portrayed by models, Miss America, Barbie dolls and screen actresses. They wear a size 5 or smaller, weigh 100 pounds and stand at a height of an average of 5'5 or above. Another statistic states that two out of five women and one out of five men would trade three to five years of their life to achieve their ideal weight. So no wonder some of us look in the mirror and scowl. The mirror just happens to show us our day to day true reality, blurry or not.

The mirror added with the audience, occasionally took a toll on my perception as a dancer and woman. Somehow my hidden phobias were pulled out from under my rug that I tried to hide. One common experience that became very apparent early in my dance career was the need for people to comment on my weight, repeatedly. What is it about weight that provokes people into commenting about a few pounds here or there? And why is the ultimate complement, "You've lost weight." Our society has become obsessed with weight, and in our field of entertainment we are suppose to uphold a certain standard, but what standard if any is realistic.

I remember I was dancing at a beautiful restaurant in Dallas, when a regular costumer told me I needed to lose 5 pounds, and then I would be perfect. I stood there looking at her with a somewhat embarrassed look on my face. All I did was nod my head and walk away. She spoke in front a large group of people, and I remember feeling very uncomfortable, vowing to lose 10 pounds. I know she had my best interest at heart, but all I heard was, "You need to lose weight." My self image took a little beating that night and what I didn't realize until now, is that I held onto these words and have kept them with me all this time. I started to wonder how many links I attached to the chain that weighs me down like an albatross, more pointedly, why did I make this part of my identity? How many of us accept negative comments that don't hold water, throwing out compliments that matter? Is this part of mass advertising along with the media and mega commercials agenda? The less sure a woman is of her self image, the more money corporations make, so the answer is obvious.

My next question is, who decided what standard belly dancers have to uphold? When I see a dancer perform, I don't see her weight performing, I see "her" performing. But this isn't how it works with many nightclubs and restaurants in regards to the type of dancers that they hire. They want dancers to be certain proportions, and visually pleasing to the eye, which can be unrealistic, unless half of us are born like our Barbie dolls. There are some restaurants that won't hire what they consider to be an overweight dancer. I know this because I have worked at a few restaurants that give lame excuses like the position has been filled. This can compromise the existing house dancers' relationship with her dance community. How do you tell another dancer she is over weight? There are certain things that most dancers just won't do. I know from experience, that weight is a personal issue, and should be addressed only if asked. Realistically, it's not totally the restaurant or house dancers fault because customers also dictate what kind of dancers they want to see. Most managers will hire belly dancers that rate within accordance to society's standards, and not women standards. So how do we as women change these so called "standards?" This is a hard question to answer, because there are so many of us dealing with the dissatisfaction of our own body image.

I think there is also the nitty-gritty that comes up with restaurant or nightclub dancing. There is a competitive rivalry that surfaces every once in awhile. I remember I thought didn't get hired at a restaurant because the house dancer interfered with my audition. She waltz over to me at the end of my audition, and told me that the owner didn't like how I looked in my costume and that I didn't get the job. She gave the impression he had her come out to talk to me, so I left disappointed, thinking maybe I needed to lose a few pounds.

A few days later, the owner called me stating that it was too bad I couldn't fit the restaurant into my schedule. He was wondering if I could at least give him one weekend a month. His statement didn't compute for a minute, but then I realized what had happened. I told him, his house dancer told me, he didn't like

57

the way I looked in my costume, eluding to the fact I wasn't hired. He laughed besides being flabbergasted at the fact his house dancer took it upon herself to create a misunderstanding, so I wouldn't dance at the restaurant. When he confronted her the following day, she did her best to lie her way out of it. Unfortunately every once in a while we all come across this type of dancer. In this instance, I decided not to dance at the restaurant even though the owner said he wanted to hire me. I just didn't want to have to work with someone who from the start wasn't trustworthy. As performers we have to pick our battles wisely, otherwise we will always be embroiled in endless fights that can be a waste of time, leading us astray from our true calling.

In some instances, our mortality hits way too close to home. I had a photo shoot with some of my students a few years ago, and realized for the first time that I was getting older. I literally saw age, staring back at me in my photographs. Living with myself day in and day out, created a blinder view of life, because I was oblivious to my aging process. My reaction to seeing the photographs surprised me the most. I was depressed for weeks, and my disposition was an imitation of Eveyore with a raincloud hovering over my head. Incidentally, not only do we have weight to contend with but along our path we meet up with age; a close relative to weight. Sometimes our stand in life, no matter how strong, can be blown over by something trivial like our ego impersonating age. Sometimes ego can keep us in denial about our age for years, until one day it just walks away laughing, leaving us confronted with the inevitable truth.

The question is, how many of us photo shop our photographs? How many of us will buy costumes that hide our problem areas? How many of us have gone on crash diets, just before we have a major performance? I have always gauged my weight according to how my costumes fit, and I have friends who do the same. When I go on a diet, the first thing I do after a few days, is put on one of my belts. So how can I feel good about my body image, if it can only look good a certain way in my costumes? We add denial into the picture which brings about a double whammy, where the ego relishes and thrives in a never ending battle. The consequences of this battle can turn into an overwhelming feeling of agitation, inflamed by the dictates of today's standards because they are not our own. The feeling is like being in a foreign country and then realizing that your passport is missing.

Sometimes looking this culprit straight in the eye, is easier said then done because most of us perform in shows where we are videotaped. As professionals, most of us want the footage of our chorography for future references and marketing. I remember a few years ago, I was videotaped in a show and I just didn't look good. I looked short and wide and for someone that stands 5'3 that can be disastrous on film, without mentioning what it did to my self esteem.

I remember getting the video from the workshop sponsor, who commented that I may not be happy with how I looked on it. Can you imagine someone telling you this, as they hand you a copy of the video, you just paid for! I went home and watched the video with my husband and daughter. They both agreed, I looked short and wide. I decide to take the video to another videographer, who thankfully resolved some of the problems. He told me the quality of the video was bad and suggested that I not use that videographer again. I told him the videographer wasn't my choice, and that the video was being sold with the problems he had just corrected. He was surprised anyone would want to sell a video that was so poorly recorded. So I learned a hard lesson, before a video can be sold with my image on it, I make sure I see it first. Since the sponsor knew the quality of the video was bad and sold it anyways, I also realized not to rely on others to look out for my best interests. This lesson taught me that making a buck can get in the way of doing the right thing. Learning the reality of this business made me aware that marketing can't just stop because we don't like how we look on film, but a heads up before the video was being sold, would have been nice.

With any video experience, consideration and respect should be a given with any show, especially when you have guest performers. With the Cleopatra's Court production, we had photographer, Pat Berrett come and take photos for both the rehearsal and evening show. One of our performers was very ill but she still performed like a pro. The photographs of her performance were very uncomplimentary, so we told the photographer to delete them. This is what you always hope for when you work with professionals; people watching your back. But sometimes, our image is stuck in a video or photograph somewhere in infamy where we look like a blob or something that could moo its way, off stage.

An American research group in 2003 said that 50 to 70 percent of normal weight women believe they are overweight. So are we trying to attain a perfect image that really exists only in our minds? In order to answer this question, I went back to the mirror and brought a magazine with me and turned the pages until I found a photograph of what I believed, was the perfect woman. I had breasts and hips... she didn't. She had a hard look to her because she was so thin. Then I realized that the image looking back at me in the mirror wasn't so bad after all. What I thought was the perfect woman turned out to be unrealistic. I mean, I picked a woman almost 6 feet tall and a hundred pounds, so what was I thinking? If we can't connect to the photos in the magazines than why do we allow these images to dictate how we should look?

"We don't need Afghan-style burquas to disappear as women. We disappear in reverse by revamping and revealing our bodies to meet externally imposed visions of ourselves." Robin Berber author and motivational speaker.

When I see dancers on stage, womanhood in all her glory must be singing to the moon and stars. I don't think as women, we understand how powerful our image is together, and what a definitive statement we make every time we move, glide and twirl on stage. The duality of our lives can lead us to live in constant contradictions outside of dance. The older I get, the more apparent it becomes that I seek sanctuary, not because I am ambiguous to my path, but because I seek justification in a safe place where I won't be judged or unmistaken in my cause. The cause is simple; accept our bodies for what they are. If this is true, then I guess I'm in constant contradiction with myself performing or otherwise.

"Self identity and self acceptance are the end result of a woman's style; it's her divine connection to the euphoric self." Leyla Najma

For a few brief moments while on stage, we have to show our audience we love who we are and mean it. The moments I cherish the most, are the ones filled with excitement, especially in the dressing rooms just before a production or show. It is electric. Granted not all my experiences have been equally memorable, but if this feeling could be put in a painting, it would be a masterpiece. So why after coming to terms with my unrealistic comparisons with magazine images, is it so hard for me to look in the mirror and appreciate what I see? Looking back at a young age, I saw that I collected and accumulated negative experiences and comments that came my way. It's a bizarre female oxymoron that becomes our habitual flawed or fractured view of ourselves. It seems to be our fate in life, to live in constant validation of negative experiences and yet it is against our very nature, to allow this adversary to dominate our lives.

In many ways, the struggle is and always has been to stand up for who I really am. In the beginning, I thought belly dance was my ally in this conflict of self identity. Yet, it seems at times, belly dance has played the devils advocate and my direction and purpose have been lost within the confusion and faltering illusions of my path. I have put a lot of issues on the shoulders of my belly dance image, and it is only fitting that at times she has buckled over with the unresolved weight of them.

If dance could be performed without the forethought of weight, I do believe we would have undefined creativity in abundance all around us.

Unfortunately in our society, women tend to hide behind the excuses of trepidation and unresolved issues with their weight. We see our flaws early in life, and they are magnified on and off the stage, without us ever showing an inch of flesh. The flaws become our validations of what is wrong with us, so our dance either heals us or exacerbates our view of how we see ourselves. We ultimately have to come to terms with the iconic woman that stands in front of the mirror. This means being naked in front of ourselves without any regrets, disillusionments or complaints. If we can see ourselves for who we really are, then our dance will showcase this renewed and elevated quality of life. Our bodies don't know how to lie, so they either reflect arrogance, disparagement and insincerity or humility, self worth and sincerity.

This led me to become curious about our image as women throughout history, so I took a look at how we have changed to become the women that we are today. Here is what I came up with; in the 1890's if you were plump and had a light complexion, you were hot (this meant you didn't work). In the early 1900's, the corset and hour glass figure were all the rage (so what if you couldn't breath). In the 1920's, if you were flat-chested and skinny, the world was your oyster! In the 50's and 60's, Marilyn Monroe ruled but Twiggy was right beside her. The 70's and 80's were all about working out and having no body fat (let's not forget about the hair). In the 90's, large breasts and narrow hips became the norm (not really). And today, women are a combination of all of the above.

As a belly dancer and woman, I can handle representing a little bit of each generation and as a matter of fact, if you look around our dance community, you will see our history alive and well in every woman. As women we have to decide what suites our own vision of beauty. And after looking at our history I realized I was in great company. So I looked back in the mirror, laughed and saw something I did like, a smile.

10 – Belly Dance Burnout

"The unknown truth of fame is like a giant ball chasing after the individual soul, keeping it from the divine slumber of creative thought."

For most dancers who are just starting out, working in restaurants and nightclubs, it is hard to ever fathom getting to a point, where you find yourself sitting on the side of the bed, trying to talk yourself into getting ready for another show. It is a reality that happens to many dancers and when it happened to me, I found there was no one to turn to. My "guilt meter" made me feel embarrassed and unappreciative thus keeping my emotions locked away.

The unknown truth is, it's not like a virus that just hits you and you can get over it. It is a gradual flu like symptom that escalates like a time bomb. Towards the end of this emotional rollercoaster, you feel like you can't get it together to perform for even the most appreciative audience. Emotions are frayed, and the littlest of things can trigger an outburst or episode of frustrated tears. Confusion, ultimately leads to a brave effort in trying to hold back emotions, in order to be the ideal and guiltless professional. I can remember talking myself into performing on weekends, when all I wanted to do, was stay home and be like a regular family person. I would create this horrible cloud that would hang over my head, and I would leave the house exhausted, resenting my good fortune and then feeling guilty for my thoughts. Somehow the entertainer in me saved the day, because I was the consummate performer that never gave in to my self-indulgence, even if it felt justified. The show always went on and I put my emotions on the back burner, trying not to sulk or, think about not being home with my family.

Dancer's who experience belly dance burn out who are in their prime, feel if they don't keep up with available opportunities, they will be replaced! I remember when this unrealistic struggle came over me, pitting the professional dancer against the Suzy homemaker in me. The professional dancer in me, felt guilty for feeling unappreciative for having work but the wife and mother in me, felt miserable because I was missing out on family time that was priceless. The worse I felt, the more I pushed myself to be super mom and belly dance aficionado. I was so busy trying to prove to myself that I could do both, that I pushed myself to the point of exhaustion. The reason why dancers feel they have to prove themselves is based on a very unrealistic truth. They end up becoming the fuel for whispers of unfair gossip and untruths being told by a few who have not clue. Whispered chatter can be like feathers that take their time, falling upon those who find themselves as topics of conversation. Before we know it, we can find ourselves tarred and feathered verbally.

The Uninvited Guests

I was dancing years ago at a restaurant in Texas, when a group of dancers came in with a legendary dancer from Egypt. My heart was pounding, because the group which consisted of 10 or more dancers, gave no warning that they were coming to watch the show. The group was polite but as my evening show came to an end, there seemed to be an unspoken indifference that was felt underneath the civil dialogue and murmurs. The indifference came from a small group at the table that made their feelings clear.

With my show over, I went to the table and talked to the director of the group, thanking her for coming to the restaurant. At that moment, I realized that not only she was unpleasant to talk to, but her curt remarks contradicted her strained and quasi courteous dialogue. It wasn't so much the words as it was her body language that told me how she felt. This type of body language is very taxing for anyone to experience. They feel like an uninvited guest that eats all the food without asking if there is enough for everyone else.

Having to prove yourself to this type of person, can become a tedious endeavor that is arduous. The best thing to do, is to stand strong and face this adversary with your own positive energy that's says, "I know who I am." At certain moments, you have to realize that not everybody is your friend and proving yourself to them is futile. So I excused myself, went to the bathroom to change out of my costume, and had a glass of wine at the owners table. I watched the group leave and waved goodbye to them. I was feeling a mixture of disappointment and antipathy because I finally realized, this is the world in which I dance in. So I looked at my empty wine glass, and asked for more wine. As I watched the restaurant owner, pour more wine, I said, "Salute". He smiled at me with a knowing look on his face and said, "Good show." I looked back at him and said, "Thank you, I needed that!" Getting up from the table he turned back around, looking at me and said, "I know."

Entertaining the Crowds

Most dancer's who are motivated to perform within the 4 to 6 year career spectrum, are ready to conquer the world. These are my favorite dancers because nothing gets them down. Most dancers at this level are motivated from an inner core of self confidence. But after awhile, life takes a toll on this inner core and self doubt seeps in slowly but surely. Why this happens, is a very important question. It is the same old story for many types of entertainment, and it has a lot to do with how much we give to our audience, and what we get back in return that sustains us. If we ask for a constant approval, this is where the dry spells can impact us the most. Our reservoir of life and vitality has to be replenished, or it will eventually diminish into a dry and barren waist land. The answer to the dry spells is simple, we have to replenish ourselves.

No matter how you look at belly dancing, this is an entertainment that affects the life of the dancer which includes family, friends, coworkers, and even the family pet. With this type of dance, life changes can be surprising, because there are so many lessons mixed in, that creates an elixir of uncertainty. The first thing that happens is the effect it has on the body image. We have to remember, that our bodies are a reflection of how we feel about ourselves. As I was working more, my body was in great shape but I noticed that my spirit was lagging behind. It was noticeable one New Years Eve, at a restaurant I danced at in Albuquerque. One of the worst snow storms we had in years came unexpectedly and suddenly that New Years, so the owner thought there might be a possibility of cancelations, resulting from the snow. But to everyone's surprise, the restaurant that night was packed. I was sitting at a back table, and realized I hadn't had a New Years Eve off in ten years. As I looked around the restaurant, it was evident that my heart was back at home. There were many reasons that brought on my melancholy, but the number one issue I struggled with, was entertaining drunk patrons. The cold weather that came with the fading light was definitely how my heart felt. Year after year, I experienced women doing a strip tease dance, trying to mimic me or men trying to grope a feel as they tried to put money down my belt. It's hard to tell a drunk that you have a tip basket, especially if they are stumbling around like a fool. After so many years of dealing with these situations, I became exhausted to the point that I lost my desire to dance publically. I knew I needed to change my dance path so I could get my mojo back, besides my joy of dancing. In other words, I needed my private space of creative bliss.

I realized that entertaining people was secondary to my needs as a person, which was at first an uncomfortable, feeling because I always put the audience first. I spent the night of the snow storm in a hotel close to the restaurant, and ended up spending more money on the hotel room than I made in tips. So that did it! I vowed to spend my next New Years with my husband, watching a movie and wearing my favorite pajamas.

Fast forward, to the following year. I was in my favorite pajamas and before the clock struck midnight I was already soundly asleep. It was the best present I had given myself in years!

I started to think about the warning signs that can emerge through time, and decided to share with you what I experienced. Looking into specific areas of belly dance burn out, made me realize that writing them down made them less threatening. In sharing these views and ideas, my hope is that it will inspire dancers to look into their own ordeals, and confront these issues head on before belly dance burn out happens. I feel if I could have foreseen certain warning signs along the way, I could have been avoided the pitfalls of belly dance burnout. Since I didn't have anyone tell me what to look for, decided to pass on what I discovered and hopefully help as many dancers, keep an eye open for these subtle changes.

Attitude Change

When we change our attitude, there seems to be one thing that we forget to change with it, and that is our perception of the world around us. Perception is very important because it helps us see the difference between the shallow aspects of our dance, to the deepest and most profound experiences. Many dancers forget that attitude can be a momentary fluctuation between having a great show, to having an off performance. If your perception and knowledge are in check and kept equal, then your attitude will follow in their footsteps.

I remember in my early years when I went to California, I was naïve and inexperienced when I started working in restaurants. My dancing had a lot to be desired in those days, but the patrons seemed to forgive my hiccups here and there. One evening, I was dancing for a full house a restaurant in the Glendale area called, Chattanooga. There is nothing like dancing for an enthusiastic audience, and for the most part, the people at this restaurant were very appreciative. On one particularly busy night, I was performing my show and by chance had my back to a large table. I was just about to turn around, when all of a sudden, a very tall blonde woman walked past me and shoved me to the floor. My music was still playing, and the crowded room went silent, waiting to see what I would do. I stood up and brushed myself off, looking around to see who knocked me down. The tall blonde was making a spectacle out of herself, so I obviously knew she was the one. Undeterred, I did what any outraged dancer would do, I grabbed a chair, put it in front of her table, stepped up on it and then started to dance just for her, and no one else. As a few minutes passed, the crowded restaurant started to laugh. Eventually, the blonde lady smiled at me and started to laugh herself. When the song came to an end, I received a huge applause from the crowd, and the blonde lady came over, tipping me $50.00 dollars. I learned that if I didn't have self respect for my dance, then I couldn't expect others to have respect for it either. It had to start with me first; my attitude had to reflect this.

Ego Crisis

Another problem that can create havoc in a dancer's world, is the ego crisis. Unfortunately, there are various types of what I call, the ego crisis that are a part of our dance scene. Identifying them helped me to lighten up and not take myself so seriously.

Type 1: This type of ego is what I call the inexperienced kind. Circumstances occur when a performer doesn't understand that they must work their way up to perform in different venues. If positions and opportunities are handed to students without merit, then they won't have any respect or appreciation for the venue itself. Teachers, who experience this type of ego crises with students, quickly learn problems can arise, especially if they don't emphasize training is a requirement to getting ahead. A gift is meaningless, if it's not earned. It's in the trial and errors of performing, that a dancer understands and learns to appreciate opportunities in front of them. Humility adds to any opportunity, because in order for a dancer to appreciate an opportunity, they have to have the humility to see it as such. The saying, *a dose of humility*, goes a long way in any show or production.

65

As a dance coach, I have experienced the ups and downs of training dancers just like with any other type of dance form. There have been solo performers I had the honor of working, with who were just amazing. The common factor in each of these particular dancers was the push to get ahead and work tirelessly in their dance training. Sometimes dancing from a creatively isolated position, cultivates the *me syndrome*. This is apart of a solo dancers journey, called the trial and tribulations of the creative self. Solo performing can foster problems, because haflas shows and venue performing is about sharing the limelight with others. Opportunities are only a chance at success, but it depends on how a performer chooses to see them. Otherwise, they are an obligation that takes time out of their busy schedules, and there is nothing worse then dealing with a impatient dancer. The obligation can weigh down any well intentioned opportunity, even if it's handed to them and as a teacher I had to learn what the word, opportunity meant. It's the chance to perform without knowing the outcome. With each earned success comes the confidence to stand out in a crowd and on the dance floor.

TYPE 2: This type of ego happens when performers get accolades early on in their career, forgetting they are in the beginning stages of learning their dance form. The mind can create hallucination of fame and fortune, hypnotizing students into thinking they hear applause everywhere they turn. All it takes is one show where the crowd responds enthusiastically, and the mind bungee jumps off into unrealistic expectations. I actually had this happen with a student, who came to me after her first dance performance at a restaurant I performed at. I offered a student night in the middle of the week, so her turn had come up to perform. She wanted to audition at the restaurant for the weekends. I was flabbergasted to say the least because she had just started to take classes with me, 7 months earlier. I stood silent and finally got out the words, "Not yet." When she argued that the audience really liked her, I reminded her that most of the audience was full of her family, who came for support. To end the debate, I decided that she needed to see what a professional dancer does on the weekends. So I had her come the following weekend to see one of my performances at the restaurant. She watched me do a thirty minute performance, ending with a drum solo. After that, she decided she needed more training.

We all want to be told how amazing and incredible we are as dancers, but the fact is, there are a lot of amazing and incredible dancers out there, who have been performing for years with a list of credentials that go on forever. But it's important to remember that compliments are a dime a dozen but experience is something you can take home to the bank.

Believe it or not, there is a flip side to the appreciative audience, and that is an indifferent crowd. If a dancer isn't experienced enough, she can find herself questioning what she once thought was an unwavering passion. I wish it was different, but compliments aren't a guarantee in this dance form, and they won't always come your way. There are moments when an audience isn't watching or interested. This is why; experience is queen so that a dancer doesn't give a half hearted performance. A seasoned dancer will look at an audience, and understand the energy, mood and then roll with the punches, making the evening enjoyable, before she ever gets out on the dance floor. Professional dancers understand that in some restaurants, we are atmosphere and not always in the forefront of the patron's attention, especially when they are eating.

I remember, I was dancing at a little restaurant in Dallas, and there were maybe four or five tables occupied in different areas. I danced one set, because the restaurant owner said it was too slow for two. I started dancing for the few tables by the windows, with only polite interest as people glanced my way. As I progressed with my show, it didn't seem like the patrons were enjoying my performance. After my show, I sat down to eat my dinner, when one of the waiters came up to me, and said he had my tip money. I actually didn't think I made any, so it was a really nice surprise. That night taught me a really good lesson, sometimes it's better to dance for your audience, without worrying about how they reacted to your dancing. Just do your best, and let the chips fall where they may. Center yourself on always being appreciative that you have the chance to perform. Remember you are continually shaping and molding your dance from within the temple of creativity. If you don't keep the fires burning inside you, there will be no sacred, creative space to center yourself from.

TYPE 3: The teaching tick is a part of the ego that can become problematic and an unfortunate factor in the studio home-base. The problem is as old as time itself, and one that has to do with human folly. It's only natural for a student's dance passion to turn into the desire to teach, but the time scale in this instance can be way off. Years of experience, can make the difference between a novice dancers realistic expectations or a distorted view on dance. Sometimes, you are looking at a fifteen year discrepancy or more, between a qualified teacher's expertise and novice's diminutive amount of time in the dance field. In our dance world, this is a reality that is starting to affect our community more and more. Consequently, we not only deal with the economic repercussions of this dance field but ethical implications, because this dance is culture based. What a novice dance teacher does, is short change the culture, history and esthetics of the dance. The best solution that I can think of is for students to ask for credentials and a bio. A professional dancer won't be offended and willingly comply to students requests.

There is another aspect to this type of problem that is slightly different, that I would like to add. There are a few teachers, who state their particular dance course or certifications will guarantee dancers/students get to a professional status within a very short period of time. This creates a new type of dancer who walks into our dance world thinking this dance form can be learned, absorbed and understood without educating themselves on its origins. This can also be called the fast food mentality, which has no place in any dance field. I know experience is golden in this dance field and patience, practice and diligence will get you farther then prematurely testing the waters before your time. A good friend said it well, "There are piranhas in the water so it's best to know where to avoid swimming when you decide to jump in."

Choreography Brain Freeze

Choreography brain freeze, not only creates repetitive, boring moves, but it can be humiliating to the experienced performer's creative image. I don't think it's uncommon for dancers who have been performing for years to experience this at one time or another; exhaustion is usually the culprit. This dance is a reflection on how we live our lives, so if we bring in our experiences, sometimes they aren't always going to be hunky dory. In order for us to keep our choreography fresh, we have to allow all experiences whether they are good or bad to seep into the mix of our creativity. Self criticism or comparing ourselves to another dancer is not only unhealthy but it will create a stagnate atmosphere. The individual, creative process can't exist in this kind of atmosphere for very long before dancers start to crack.

Remember there is only one of you in the Universe and what a true blessing you are. Your creativity is already unique because "*you*" exist. Also remember that becoming someone else's carbon copy or imitating another dancer may seem like a compliment, but it takes away from your own creative process. Dancers need to perform from their own place of reflection in life. We all have our own treasure trove of moves. We have to look inside ourselves for those jewels placed along with our gold and silver inspirations.

I experienced choreography blocks my first five years of performing, and I remember the frustration of feeling isolated from my dance. I wondered why other dancers could create beautiful choreographies, and I was left barren of ideas. It wasn't so much that my treasure trove of moves weren't within reach; it's the fact that I didn't learn how to implement choreography basics that made sense to me. I learned various choreographies in dance classes, but I didn't understand the fundamentals of why certain moves and combinations were placed in music. The rudimentary basics of Choreography 101, need to be taught in a way that makes sense to the common dancer. I'm a trial by error type of dancer, so I learn best by implementing what I like first and then seeing how it fits. I can't stress enough, that making choreography accessible in an easy to understand step by step method will change how dancers understand the creative process. Dancers need a way where they can visualize movement to music in an environment that makes it effortless and easy to understand. The experienced and top professional dancers are priceless in this area, which is why you can't bottle and pass off inexperience in this dance field. The end result says it all.

With the tests of time, I finally understood the structure and methodology of how to put my choreographies together but I must admit I struggled. Students need creative license to work on choreographies as they understand the movements in their bodies. If choreographies are implemented as weekly homework, than this will help the students understand choreography and the structure and connection of the studio curriculum. This also helps to develop self confidence within the student, so she can find her own creative inspiration and work with it.

The Professional "No Time" Problem

Time management is something that affects most dancers, whether they are professionals or amateurs. One of the first signs of this unsuspecting and sly problem is the inclination to perform more and practice less. Most professional dancers who are in demand focus on the next performance or gig, incorporating practice when time permits. I'm not saying professional dancers don't practice, but solo performers can juggle multiple shows within a short time-span. The unthinkable can happen, where gradually, performances can suffer do to repetitive, halfhearted efforts that drain any dancer's enthusiasm. As a performer, it's hard to be enthusiastic for the audience 24/7 without exhaustion starting to show in performances. Dance isn't just about performing and training, it's about being human with all our frailties. As my career progressed, it became clear that not only was I exhausted, but I didn't want to practice the following two days after a full weekend of dancing. I made up excuses, telling myself I had valid reasons why I didn't have the time to practice. No one told me this happens, or talked to me about the weekly ping pong match that entered my head. One side was represented by guilt and the other by exhaustion. The results for each week varied. I couldn't tell who would win but I knew there was no way to wager on either side, because they were both unpredictable and equally compelling.

Sometimes a gig can come along that seems too good to pass up, but even though we know we should pass on it, we say to ourselves, we'll pass on the next one. The next one comes along and we go through the same scenario all over again. The emotional rollercoaster can feel like plummeting down an incline with no brakes. I noticed I missed out on family get-togethers and home cooked meals.

The straw that broke the camels back was when I danced at a restaurant during my anniversary. The restaurant owner said a group of people had specifically asked for me, and he was adamant that I to dance that evening. Fortunately, my husband agreed to celebrate our anniversary at the restaurant, but secretly, I felt like I sold out for a few measly dollars. After that, I vowed never to perform on my anniversary again, unless it was by my husband's request. Like most professional dancers, my private life slowly took a back seat to my career. There can be a high mortality rate in broken relationships and marriages. Ultimately, there is no gig worth the price we pay with our private lives. It's important to remember, that once we say yes to a gig and no to our family, it's time lost forever.

69

Performing can become so addictive, that we have to choose what kind of family life we want to preserve. We may live to dance but we have to remember that living also means experiencing life outside the stage. Our lives with family and friends in many ways add to our creativity giving us reasons to dance, so our family is up on stage with us too.

The Unresponsive Audience

The unresponsive audience doesn't help in the confidence arena, and they can undermine the moral of any seasoned performer. For various people who aren't educated in our dance form, confusion, misunderstandings and wrong impressions take the place of intelligent questions. Inexperience in front of different types of crowds can be devastating to performers.

If it was as easy as psychically finding out what type of audience we are dancing for before hand, then this wouldn't even be a topic. I have asked every question imaginable to event coordinators and customers, to ensure a good show. Sometimes being informed ahead of time isn't enough, because I've encountered unfounded prejudices even with all my positive efforts put forward. There are people who feel they are well informed based on media and tabloid information, ignoring the facts that are in front of them. We can't let a few bad apples ruin a night of dance and good fun, so it's best to just ignore them as best you can.

Let's face it, there are times when we have danced and the audience's response was luke warm. It's so hard not to beat ourselves up, because most of us use the audience as our performance gauge. Our gauge needs to be how we feel inside while we're performing, and only in this should we trust the truth of our achievements. Our gut will always tell us the truth. We have to learn from our own truth, so that in the future, we can make better choices based on self evaluation. Understanding ourselves is the best ammunition we can have to ensure that on our end, we did our best.

I remember dancing for an audience in a small town in Texas that was the ultimate dead pan audience. I tried smiling at a few people in the front rows, but it was to no avail. I felt bad for the other dancers because I could tell they were just as uncomfortable as I was. I asked the hostess what was up with the audience, and she said they were always like that. "You mean they have been to workshop shows before?" I asked in an exasperated voice. "This is just the way they are here." She said in a matter of fact manner. The applause was polite for each of us, but surprisingly towards the end of the show, there were quite a few people who waited to have their pictures taken with us. As I've said before, you can never judge your performance based on the audience's response. The entertainers faux pas will always be the audience, because we wager too much of ourselves on how they react to our creativity.

It sounds cliché but second guessing ourselves just adds fuel to the fire of self doubt. All performers have an advantage before they ever get in front of an audience. This one advantage is the fact that the story they tell, is one of a kind. Remembering who we are is a constant affirmation that dancing is about how we react to life. So when the feeling of belly dance burn out starts to happen, just remember that we not only remind the masses that life is a miracle, but we remind ourselves, every time we perform on stage.

11 - Belly Dance and the Feminine Image

"There is no better way to express our dance then by embracing who we are and dancing with the veils of our choice."

History shows us through paintings, that the veil came to symbolize the untouchable and tantalizing appeal of women in the Middle East. To show just a little part of the body, was alluring enough to cause men to pine for women's affection. If we look at 19th Century paintings, of various scenes of women dancing, the look of the belly dancer is quite refined. The distinctive folds in the belt, or the accessories from the ankle, all the way up to the headpiece, tell the individual story of each dancer. This is how dancers from the past to the present, set themselves apart from their counterparts. I can remember seeing the movie, "Cleopatra," starring Elizabeth Taylor for the first time and thinking, how beautiful the costumes were and how much fun they would be to dance in. "Samson and Delilah" with Hedy Lamarr, is my all time favorite Biblical movie and her costumes inspire me even to this day. Looking at Claudette Colbert's costumes in the 1934 "Cleopatra," they look like modern costumes of today.

Hollywood has very unusual ideas about what women from the Middle East wore. But if we look back through the ages of time, the belly dance costume hasn't really changed that much. This really surprised me, because as I was exploring our history, it became apparent to me that when you have a good design, it's not only hard to improve on it, but it magically reinvents itself time and again.

Years ago, I was asked to dance in an Asian Festival which was a huge honor for me. I remember walking into the dressing room, and being greeted with the vibrant beauty of so many women, dressed in unusual costumes, that were foreign to me. The dresses, varied in color, and their designs dazzled my senses, transfixing me on the spot. With their costumes speaking to me in ancient whispers, I have to admit, that I felt a little out of place in my cabaret costume.

Their movements were very subtle and their gestures very soft and poetic, which made me wonder what kind of poetry belly dancing would be in comparison? When it was time for me to perform, I realized that our music says a lot about our image. Every aspect of our costumes and music, convey captivating images that intertwine with our dance. My costume was like magic, because it made me feel free enough to dance my story within movements and gestures that spoke to the audience. For some reason, I wanted to relate with the audience, a desire for them to see my dance as the ancient mother, serious and respected. But I have to question why I even felt the need to defend my dance form. The dancers with their enveloped movements almost seemed to speak to me teasingly, asking me why I wasn't covered more. Maybe I was just hearing my own voice questioning this since my costume revealed more skin then theirs.

After I finished my dance, the response was overwhelming. It was unequivocally clear that the distinct differences of my music and costume, guided the audience to an appreciative direction regarding the culture I represented. Costuming and music really make the difference for people. It's almost as if the audience could see the cultural aspects of my story within each movement, all the while watching my costume accent each word being danced with my body. With that experience, I finally understood how important the differences are in cultural dress, music, history and style for the audience.

Years ago when I was in Cairo, Egypt, I was able to see the legendary belly dancer, Zuhair Zaki perform live and as I look back, I realize how lucky I was, to have seen such a legend perform. Zuhair Zaki is the total sum of what the belly dance image is for me. Every movement told a story, and helped me "hear" the music. I was taught a very good lesson that night, because I saw what a masterful dancer can do with music. I also saw Zuhair Zaki become the essence of belly dance as she performed. It wouldn't have mattered what she wore or where she was, the spirit of the dance was in her. I could see and feel belly dance to such a degree, that I felt the Goddess, Isis herself in the room. At that moment, the ancient Egyptian temples, hieroglyphs, and Pharaonic history came alive. As Zuhair felt the music, I felt it with her. These are those spiritual moments that change you forever!

A few weeks later, I saw another famous belly dancer, Dina perform and was totally surprised at the sexual innuendos that emanated from her dance. The image of belly dance changed that night for me, because I had assumed that provocative gestures were not allowed. But somehow, Dina made it work for her and as I watched her performance, I saw that she was teasing the audience, leading them into her dance. It was fun to watch her play up on the audience without losing her integrity. Her sexuality never got in the way of her performance. It enhanced her movements, and I understood at that moment, that Dina chose to dance free of any inhibitions or restraints, her world put on her.

As a modern woman, I often wonder how close my image is to women back hundreds of years. Our evolution as women has never been more evident than in the belly dance world. As a little girl, I heard about the dance of the seven veils, and I always imagined the veils as vibrant colors, symbolizing the rainbow. As I became older I realized that the dance represented life from the eyes of our feminine image. If we look at the true meaning of this dance, the removal of the veils represent seven earthly illusions that fall away with each veil. In order for us to become the total feminine archetype in myth, these veils must fall from us so we can transcend into individual interpretations of the Goddess. As with all myths, I wondered what these seven veils of illusion were, because I have a suspicion that we may still be portrayed within these myths today. It became apparent to me that each illusion had an opposite side to it, so here's my version of the seven illusions.

1. **The Virgin-Temptress**

Many dancers have both abilities to enchant their audiences by offering the untouchable innocence of movement combined with eye contact that teases with a fleeting look.

2. **Intrigue-Deception**

The ability to captivate our audience is a major part of our story telling but with all stories we must tell the audience that what intrigues them is only an illusion. This in itself can be perceived as a deception because we work so hard on the illusion that at moments it may become real.

3. **Mother-Sex Goddess**

Both of these describe the dilemma all women come across through out their careers. While we dance as women who understand what it means to carry and give life we are also expected to be proficient in the art of love. The illusion for most people is that we can be both but they want the two separate.

4. **Wise Woman-Childlike Innocence**

The knowledge a dancer puts in her performing sets her apart from the average dancer. Knowledge is power and our movements speak volumes in regards to our history. The illusion here is that while we dance with experience our audiences to a certain degree want a virtuous dancer that will give them an unsullied look at our dance.

5. **Wife-Mistress**

In our dance we are compelled to perform from places of the heart. At least some of our music has this impassioned theme in certain songs. As women we feel the need to complete ourselves which is why we search for our mate. The mistress on the other hand is compelled to search outside of this completion which in itself is the wife's mirror opposite. We distance ourselves from the mistress personification yet in the eyes of our admirers the hope is that they get a glimpse of her.

6. **Muse-Transmutation**

Poetry and music speak of the dancer that takes her audience to places of sublime heights. As dancers we are the muses of our times. At the same time we experience the audience that doesn't understand our dance and they try to alter it to fit their perception of the world. We than become a misunderstood version of our own poetry.

7. **Diva-Modest Maid**

A dancers self confidence has to come across to the audience or they will be sorely disappointed. Many fans expect a confident woman during and after shows. Yet I have found that dancers can almost believe too much in their personas that they create. We can get caught up in this illusion just as much as anybody. The catch here is to know when to turn your dance persona on and off.

As belly dancers we inspire so much in people, and our allure isn't just the pretty costume, it is what we signify as women. My question is, do we understand what it is that we represent for so many? I have worked with a few women who were disassociated from their body image and I have been there myself. It's hard for any of us to have a clue regarding beauty especially if we buy into mixed messages from the media and cultural attitudes. With the contradiction of self acceptance versus self loathing, how comfortable are we as a community being in the position of the feminine archetype for today's women? If we can't get past the door of self appreciation, than I don't see us in the forefront of today's feminine society.

We are immeasurable as women especially within the dance form itself. Our dance helps us create our own personal dairy full of myths, fantasy and reality, all mixed together so that we can emerge into our own feminine image. But the difference here is that we reawaken a part of ourselves that not only enhances our self image, but allows us to appreciate our path.

I have often wondered, after creating our feminine image, do we then transform gradually into her. Isn't this really what belly dance does? We heal and then become the women we are intended to be. This is how I believe the essence of belly dance lives and thrives, through each generation of women. If we can understand our own image, than we can be living examples of what belly dance is, and the veils of illusion then become nothing more, then invisible restraints that disappear through our own transformation. In this sense we are reborn into women, who are comfortable in their own body, mind and spirit. And there is no better way to express our dance then by embracing who we are and dancing with veils of our choice.

12 - The Introspective Belly Ache

"Introspection is an interesting thing to experience because it brings out our thoughts we put away on a shelf called, undisclosed."

The Female Tick

There is so much to be said about being in the company of women, as a woman. The disingenuous nature of women could make for a great fictional novel, based on real life experiences. If drama is written in an off chance novel, its ambiguous details are easier to swallow. As it stands, women walk in fractured disguises that shadow their true sense of worth, creating splintering conclusions regarding their competition. At any given time we become the target of our own gender, based on an unrealistic measuring stick of assumptions and insinuations.

Because of this, I have come across something very interesting that I call the *female tick*. It's something that became more prevalent as time went by. The definition of a tick, *is a mark or to indicate something*. I find this very interesting, because one side effect of the *female tick* is a condition within our community that really does indicate an unhealthy manner of communicating with each other. Since belly dance attracts a majority of women, drama seems to follow, lurking around the corner just waiting for a chance to happen. Thus the relationship between women and drama creates the female tick. On the other side of the infamous "tick", we have creativity in all her glory. This relationship is the inspiration that takes place, in order to create shows and dance plays that otherwise would not exist. What I find interesting, is when creativity happens, we get a little bit of everything mixed in. It all formulates an integral part of making our unique recipe an elixir, that changes the way we see, view, breathe belly dance. The deciding factor on the outcome of any performance is based on a dancer's state of mind and how she accepts her image. A self created flaw tends to magnify itself ten fold, consequently changing a dancer into a mirror opposite of her own irrational fears. The elixir can become quite a brew.

I often wonder how women treated each other in Harems, and if we have progressed in our rapport with each other or if there is still a consistent pattern of competitive rivalry that has lodged itself into our genetic makeup?

I eagerly look to strong women figures in history and movies, for answers to the female tick. Mae West, created a niche for herself that embodied the strong feminine archetype that could survive anything, even the typical typecasting of women in her day. Is the *female tick* a typecast that we just bought into because we forgot who we are as women, or is it that our history was written in for us so we wouldn't know the difference? In the end, I have realized that it is so much easier to look at a fairy tales or romantic characters created for the screen or novels, then to look for validation in the world around me. That is why, to be within the dance world's walls, full of the aroma of perfumes and the visual array of fabrics, coins and bling with the echoes of distant drums mixed together, is so alluring. The senses almost go through an agonizing withdrawal, living in the outside world and because of it, our homes turn into our Bedouin counterparts and refuge.

As the eternal circle of time swallows up my youth, I have found that I hastily evaluate and measure my passion and position in life. Dance seems to make one half of me immortal, and the other half mortal. The two sides make for awkward company within my minds eye, and I wonder if this is the same for my community? I have found that this double sided, quandary, is endless and full of unknown sentiments that sneak up on me out of nowhere. I will confess that I can't totally blame typecasting for all the woes of the belly dance world.

Caution Buttons

Within the years of traveling along my belly dance path, I have come across experiences that on the learning scale have sent me on an emotional rollercoaster. It's amazing how emotions can escalated beyond the imaginary horizon, and then spiral to a plummeting low, full of dark and disturbing impressions. From the school of hard knocks, I tend to evaluate the world according to what happens to me, forgetting to look at how an issue relates to me first. It's like I habitually react to things, instead of evaluating it according to its initial importance. Belly dance seems to be a button that brings out the reactive side of me, one that automatically defends my position or point of view before I can actually see what the issue is. I have witnessed women take a stand, defending a particular friend's point of view, based on no further information beyond what they heard. I think we have all witnessed and done this, so I'm the pot calling the kettle black; I include myself in this as well.

As I observe in how women relate to each other, it seems easier to place rivalries in a mental compartment that says "caution." This way, we don't have to be friends with suspicious people because we already have an excuse to make sure our vigilant opinions stick. It seems easier to keep insecure feelings alive, but immobile while we attach a button to them that can be pushed at a moments notice. The female conspiracy theory, can exist until we come to terms with our own inadequacies. There comes a time, in our life journey, where we have to face our own delusions and learn how to see ourselves without our self portrayed flaws.

I have found that since I have put myself out in the public eye, it is a common occurrence to have some people come back and poke me in the eye, without hesitation or warning. Maybe the button is a defensive mechanism, created so that I don't go blind and at the same time, it causes me to feel safe in uncertain circumstances. We try to wear our life in a way that doesn't show the wear and tear of our experiences, but yet, without warning, our insecurities can become the detail of who we are, with a Liberace flare. This is the moment the drama queen appears out of nowhere, and materializes to the outside world, like magic.

At various points in our lives, we can forget that we are only wearing an appearance and not living one.

Performers seem to go the full gamut in the spectrum of emotions, insecure to assured, when appeasing the masses with their creative talent. I know for myself that negative feedback can put me in a funk, even though I know it will help me in the long run. In the immediate scope of things, my emotions are fragile but at the end of the emotional let down, I experience a gain in strength and the creative process starts all over again. So I wonder what it is about women, who without a moments notice, criticize another person's artistic process, all the while defending their own right to create. Can we all get along or is this unrealistic, especially since historically it seems, women's identities have been put into distorted, boxed in versions of themselves from a multitude of cultural and social dictates. In saying this, I am reminded of past experiences that left me wishing I would have been born with fast thinking, articulate brilliance. To say the right thing or have a come back at a moments notice was passed by me to my eloquent sister.

Not only did Picasso get us right, he probably went crazy from looking at our skewed and distorted images, we reveal at any given moment. The view of who we are has to be perceived in the detail of our essence, otherwise our image can become blurry and distorted even to us. Our perception of who we are shows itself in our choices, opinions and reactions to the day to day conversations that materialize with a conscious nudge we have with ourselves. I don't want to think I have an eye on the side of my face, but sometimes after a misunderstanding, my Ms. Potato head parts pop out and appear to be replaced without any forethought as to where they originally belong.

In the world of women, it seems that there is this amazing ability to turn friendship into an animosity with such haste, that I often wonder what is in our nature that makes us turn on each other so quickly. Perhaps it's in our nature to judge each other, according to how we've been treated ourselves. But the "*female tick*" is a little more vicious than this. The *female tick's* instability is like an earthquake zone, that leaves those who survive her anxious and uncertain on how to handle her after shocks. The emotional upheavals can come in an instant, with no warning. But the remaining lesson isn't always easy to see, because within each friendship, sometimes learning the lesson isn't enough to retain the friendship or repair it. This problem has to do with the "caution" button that is created once we feel a boundary has been stepped over. The easier solution is to get rid of buttons entirely, so there's nothing to push. They can become a nuisance after awhile anyways, because before you know it, they can mysteriously multiply on their own. It can be like a Pandora's Box, resulting in a world full of dancers, carrying around buttons, targeting each other all over the place.

Being creative is a very spiritual and rewarding experience, so it would only make sense for us to take a good look at our dance communities principles and values, to make sure "caution" buttons are a thing of the past. Eventually, we have to come up with a solution at least for ourselves, so that our dance journey is a testament to our personal growth. We can't allow our focus and aspirations to be effected, and derailed, languishing over others negativity. Focus is key here, because without it, we would forget our journey's purpose all together. Lessons are learned the easy way or the hard way; there never seems to be an in between.

We just need to remember, there is always a reference point called the feminine image. With her ancient history, we have our own GPS (Goddess, Purpose and Strength).

Heads Up

I thought I would bring to light, a few problem areas that have stumped me on occasion, and I know they are common place for many of us. If anything, this will give newbie's or beginner-intermediate dancers a heads up.

There seems to be two kinds of dancer's that work together. The first are, the die hard professionals who live to dance, and the second are, the professional hobbyists who dance when they can. Conflict can occur when certain dancers carry most of the work load. A hazy or unclear predicament can arise when dancers agree to participate in shows or venues. Ultimately the unforeseen agenda becomes immediate and explanations regarding job or family obligations interrupt commitments. Equal efforts of distribution and preparation as many unsuspecting dancers have found out, has nothing to do with the word equal. It's only natural for a feeling of warranted resentment to arise amongst those who are doing most of the work against those who are giving a token effort. It's a given that jobs are necessary in paying the bills, but for some dancers making a living with their dance, it pays their bills.

I love to dance, but I understand that this is my business and there has to be a professional vibe brought to the table, otherwise an atmosphere of unprofessionalism will not only permeate the air but affect relationships left and right. The obvious issue is following through with ones word whether you are a hobbyist or professional. I think fear is another factor that can play with people's heads. Wanting to perform is different then having to perform. If people don't have a tenacity that makes them want to strive to climb higher, then they will always stay at a mediocre level. Because of this, I enjoy working with professionals or professional hobbyists because the end result usually raises the bar of professionalism. Mediocrity can't exist within a group that intends excellence and in the end, achieves it.

The Bloat Fish Syndrome

Another interesting predicament is what I call, the *bloat fish* syndrome. I have come to realize that this dance form can be a blessing and a curse at the same time. It really is an interesting testing ground for deep rooted insecurities that are swept under the rug, made of unrealized or unachieved goals. The ego can be inflated to compensate for apparent imperfections that reflect back our image like a bizarre house of mirrors. No matter how distorted or deformed our ideals are, most women won't show them to the outside world. But this isn't healthy because bottling up insecurities, just creates a false sense of empowerment that is based on a very fragile foundation. If we expect dance to compensate for what we lack in life, we off set the balance of what its true purpose is and that is to exist for joy, creative purity or in one simple word, **bliss**. The people that I have encountered who have the *bloat fish syndrome* are masters of anonymity and deception. It's only human to invent our own enigma but the danger is in believing that what we create to a point of becoming trapped in our own delusion.

If communication is based on dealing with a certain amount of delusions, it's no wonder relationships can become precarious, because there is no way to know what lurks underneath any one person's foundation. What stirs the soul can be a very unique and individual response to our view of the world but even more so, because it can say so much regarding how we feel about each other. The mere fact that we have so much in common makes me wonder why we evaluate what is so different about each other. If we saw more similarities with each other, there wouldn't be this need to have a separatist or alienated reaction to each other.

Unfortunately, typecasting can play a part in how we delegate with each other. If we don't question what doesn't work in our community, I don't see changes coming any time soon. So the question remains, what is it that needs to change? What type of communication do we need to have that will give us a sense of feminine empowerment, with a combined synergy that we can all feel apart of? Realistically, I know not everyone will see eye to eye but if we can have some common ground our common goals will start off in a new direction of unity that inadvertently strengthens our community as a whole.

13 – Photography & the Sexual Self

"Photography enhances the essence of who we are as women because it captures live our individual truth; the allure of our sensual and sexual self."

What kinds of photographs draw you into a website or photo gallery? As a website owner, it's necessary that I change and update my website because it's essential to good traffic. Students need to visually see that as a family business, we are changing with technology, so new videos, websites, photos and dialogue, showcase our business ideals and methodologies keeping dancers informed.

Photographs are a major investment for me because there are so many things I can do with them. But how many dancers understand this investment and address the issue of spending money on photographs, as necessary? As professional dancers, it is so important to upgrade portfolios with yearly photographs, so people can connect growth and success visually with your image. Besides, photographs illustrating various reviews of the different stages in a dancer's career, they bring the fantasy aspect of the dance, upfront and personal to fans and admirers. They also connect us to our history and to our community, in ways words can't. There's a saying that states a picture is worth a thousand words so what would your prose be like and what would your verse say? How would history place together different and individual depictions of belly dance? It's easy to see that belly dance photographs could create a whole new fad on what sexy is. Each dance generation has their look that represents the mind frame and issues of their time. And because of this, photography can parallel our history showing us how far we have come and how far we still have to go. Either way, women have always had the ability to mix drama into history especially when it comes to posing for photos or paintings. There are a multitude of reasons why we photograph ourselves, most noticeably to discover some part of ourselves that has been hidden. Is it empowerment caught forever in a photo or is it a moment where we allow ourselves to be sensual women? An image can provoke many emotions within society, even within ourselves. The big question is, what responsibility do we have to society to represent an image that is acceptable and respectable? The belly dance costume throughout history has become a symbol, portraying us as the seductress or temptress. Let's look at Salome for example. The chance that she "belly danced" was slim because of the etiquette of her day and dancing like she is portrayed in movies would have ruined her chances for marriage. Belly dance, through history became an accessory with Salome, when in fact her dance style would have been more acrobatic. My point is that many artists through out history have painted the famous scene of Salome dancing, which ultimately made her the symbol of seduction within our dance. So a painting or photograph can be a powerful influence on the minds of society. This can also lead us to contradictions regarding our own image. How can we have a respectable image when our legacy is already tainted?

If you look at Mata Hari, she was a woman ahead of her time but she also paid the price for her eccentric and bold behavior. Are we still paying the same price to this day, maybe more understated? If Mata Hari knew her demise would she have continued life as usual? Would any of us today change how we present ourselves, if we knew the cost down the line? It became apparent to me, that our dance image is not only perceived by us but influenced by how society sees our dance. The two don't always mix well. At the same time we are controlled by society's standards and I have always felt this is where the misconception of the dance began. So perhaps photographs in their own way, help us change these misconceptions, because we boldly take on the dictates of society through photographs. Photographs in their way can do the impossible by taking on the problem and solving it, twofold. It's a natural way of taking on the prejudice of our dance and helping us become uninhibited, finding our own sense self.

Modern Day Cleopatra

A few years ago, my first foray with photographs became a fun and inventive way for me to impersonate famous women that I admired. Front and center was the total embodiment of woman; Cleopatra. I found this particular photo shoot a milestone because I grew up having read that Cleopatra was able to seduce a man without showing an inch of flesh. Don't' we all wonder if we might have this ability? So I decided I wanted to be a modern day Cleopatra, creating my version of her or a sexy vixen of today. As the first photos were taken, I felt a sense of empowerment that came from knowing I was for the most part, in charge of how I came across on camera. I was lucky; my photographer friend Jeff had an amazing way of making me comfortable in my own skin. Towards the end of the photo shoot, I was lying down on the floor that was covered with veils. I casually looked up at Jeff when he said, "Wait a minute. Don't move." My impromptu position became the shot we had both been working towards for hours. Fortunately, Jeff understood what I was trying to recreate and he also understood my personality, so I didn't get totally lost in Cleopatra's likeness, I kept some of me in the image.

Cleopatra is the one woman ruler in history that embodies all the elements that most women strive to achieve or at least have fun trying. Her name alone can cause the imagination to run wild. This is the same reaction we want people to have when they see our photographs. If you look at websites and magazines, there are varieties of photographs of many dancers in provocative poses. A dancer can convey many messages with her body positioning which can lead the viewer to think her message isn't just sensual but sexual. Because photographs get across a certain messages to viewers, what happens when the message is portrayed in a well thought out photograph and the end result is not sensual but sexual? Where does sensuality and sexuality cross? The definition of sensuality is the capacity for enjoying the pleasures of the senses. The definition of sexuality is the state of being sexual. So what if the two were combined together, then that would mean that we enjoy our sense of being sexual. Cleopatra was aware of her sexual influence and as a woman ruler she used this to her advantage. In our day and age we try to emulate her because for many of us, Cleopatra signifies the true essence of womanhood.

Isadora Duncan was by any standards ahead of her time in regards to her many relationships. In viewing her photographs, I would have to say the one thing I noticed about Isadora Duncan, is that her personal life never showed in her photos and she was a true artist to the end (tragic as it was). Her message was never misunderstood just like with Cleopatra. The difference is one used her sexuality and the other used her sensuality. Either way both women whether in paintings or photographs, depict images that invoke women from all over the world to try to emulate them. We obviously want a little bit of both when we create an image for our fans. Sometimes within that special photo, our essence seeps through, immortalized for all time thus showing a small piece of our feminine image.

Egyptian Desert

For my next adventure in photography, I decided to pose as the young Pharaoh Tutankhamen's wife, Ankhesenamun. The movie, *The Mummy* inspired this photo shoot and I was fortunate enough to be photographed by my friend Pat Berrett. I was body painted resembling Ankhesenamun in the movie, by Pam Trent. By the time she was done, I not only felt like a Queen but I looked like one. Pat and I went out to a desert oasis, thirty minutes out of town and he photographed me in the gorgeous afternoon light just before dusk. I stood upon these amazing sand dunes with this bronze body paint all over me, feeling Egypt herself was with me, time immortal. Impersonating two Egyptian queens within the span of two photo-shoots was ultimately the best decision I ever made. The fact that I was connected to two women of influence and power, bolstered my self esteem by leaps and bounds. In many ways, I feel we become symbolic of immortal women for our fans. In our field of entertainment, it's not just about being a representative of women today, but incorporating the past by keeping it alive in our image.

After about three weeks, I invited Pat and Pam to dinner to celebrate our successful photo shoot. We went to a local pizzeria that is a favorite amongst the college students in the downtown area. We were standing in line to be seated, when a dance acquaintance of mine walked up to me and said she had heard about my "naked" photo shoot. I introduced her to Pat and Pam then asked her, "What naked photo shoot?" She said she heard through the grapevine that I had done a naked photo shoot. I laughed and told her, I had body paint on along with an Egyptian belt. We were all amazed at how fast the news got around, especially since I only mentioned it to two people. It was one of the best decisions of my dance career and it sparked an interest in body painting thereafter in my dance community.

Our individual images in photographs are a big part in selling our dance ability to the masses. The artistry behind creating any image is essential in having photographs that impact our target market. So in the end, we are selling our dance ability and our image and packaging them in a way, where we give the impression that we are the embodiment of success.

How far can any belly dancer push her image and make it acceptable, not only for her community but for the outside world? If too much sexuality is shown in a photograph, it affects how people see a dancers marketing intention. Opinions can be formulated, based on an image within an instant based on individual concepts and hang ups. There can be so much insinuated in a pose, like a seductive look can imply something that never crossed the mind of the dancer. So what a dancer says in a photograph is powerful and can affect many people, even in ways she never expected. Sometimes, images come alive the way life happens, spontaneously and unexpectedly.

I have often wondered with all the great photographers out there, why dancers don't use photographs to show the world what they are up to. If a dancer or troupe is advertising a show and I can't go, I usually look forward checking out the photographs of the event. There is a statement communicated to each and every person looking at your photos. Photographs bring this statement right into a dancer's home. So, I found that investing in photographs and working with good photographers helped me create a wonderful archive of photographs that are not only fun to look at, but give my dance history to family and friends.

Let's face it, society can create a double standard for anything it wants. Back in the 1960's and 1970's the belly dance LP covers, were very provocative, especially in regards to the poses of many of the belly dancers. Some of the costumes had slits up both thighs with just a hint of material coming down the middle covering the crotch area. They seemed uninhibited, showing a lot of skin along with see through skirts. There is even a dancer with Tassels instead of a bra with a barely there skirt. It's evident that our fashion sense has changed through out the years, but when it comes to provocative poses, sultry looks and come-hither glances, the question remains, have we changed any?

Censorship changes along with history, which makes it harder for us to distinguish between our unadulterated view of being women or the provocative temptress, because of restrictions imposed on our image. As women in a very unique and ancient dance form, it's important to show in photography, how we have changed through out history. Photographs are "our" lineage and they show the world who we are. Perhaps, because of issues with self image and the Playboy era, we have wanted to say, "We are different." We don't have to take our clothes off in photographs to get across that we are sensual and sexual women. So perhaps without knowing it, we have taken all of our trials and tribulations as women and found the perfect outlet to express our feelings and thoughts about the world around us.

Photographs that capture emotion through movement, poses and attitude, become timeless and a way we make "our" mark on the world. When I'm on stage or in front of a camera, I often feel naked because all aspects of me are expressed and exposed through my movements. What is revealed are the parts of me that I hide away from society and keep to myself. So my image on stage is many things, including the sensual and sexual self. Today, I have found peace with both so consequently my photographs show the viewer the woman that I have become, and the dance that I represent. Photography shows how comfortable I am with myself. So do we critique photographs by how comfortable or uncomfortable we are with our own body image? It's only natural to do so. In the end, how we view photography says a lot about how we feel about ourselves. Since my body is a representation of my life impression, I'm letting the world know there is more to me than meets the eye. I don't want to show my vulnerability in photos yet in many ways, photographs show all of my insecurities of that moment. I have always felt that photographs should show our fans a little of who we are, but only a glimpse. The rest should be left to their imaginations because in many ways, this is what keeps us alive and working. Our fans need this allowance to imagine what they think we are, especially if our image is their refuge from everyday reality.

This brings to question, why do dancers use photographs from 10 to 20 years ago? Since my photographs are a story board of my career I want people to see how I have grown in my dance. Photographs need to tell the truth about what a dancer looks like not from twenty years ago. As performers it's our job to stay in shape and look our best. I am a very different dancer now than I was 20 years ago. My photographs from back then show my inexperience. I have a relaxed and secure look to me now. When people look at my photographs, I want them to see a professional dancer with years of experience under her belt. At the same time, I don't want them disappointed because I am older than what my photos show. It seems gender based that age is our enemy, so photos from 20 years ago stay on the forefront of many dancers' websites. We must look for ourselves in the mirror and make peace with what we see.

The Bra That Wasn't

Since I use my photographs as a part of my marketing strategy, it makes sense that I create ways to build up my own image. But I have to tell you, in my early days, I had no clue how to make my image work for me. I'll never forget one of my first photo shoots I had years ago. I had a favorite pink costume, but unfortunately the bra was way too big for me. At the time I was a B cup. So as you can imagine, people would do a double take after watching me dance on stage with my stuffed bra and then see me walking around in my cocktail dress. Ok, it was dumb on my part, but I really didn't take into consideration the important of a good fitting costume.

Months after I bought the pink costume, I hired a local photographer to take professional photos of me in it. From the get go, I noticed he said nothing in regards to how I looked, make up or lighting. Because of the time of day he was photographing me in, the costume didn't look right in the outside light. Needless to say, I learned a lot with that photographer. The first lesson I learned, was to choose a more interactive photographer. Secondly, I had to understand what time of day was best for shooting outdoors. Last but not least, I had to make sure my costumes fit appropriately. To my horror with the amount of make up I had on, I could have given Frankenstein's bride a run for her money! After the shock of seeing the photographs, I had my bra cut down to fit my "actual" size. I realized shocking people wasn't part of the image I wanted to portray.

The unfortunate thing here is that the photographer didn't communicate with me at all, and I didn't know enough at the time to talk with him in advance. It sticks in my mind as the one photo shoot that definitely showed not only my inexperience, but the photographers. Needless to say, I burned all the photos!

Group Photography; Herding Cats

Working with a photographer solo is one thing, but bringing in students into a photo shoot can create a mix of excited chaos. It's just the way it is with the energy of women which includes grandiose expectations and insecurities. In the beginning, I found out it isn't always easy to get arms and legs positioned in a group photograph which works to everybody's advantage. There is always one person who blinks, twitches and bends a leg or arm in a way that overshadows everybody else's perfect pose. The more dancers there are in a shot, the more chances of Murphy's Law. Adding to this, I learned that nothing works out exactly the way we see it in our mind and with group photography the outcome is a roll of the dice. The reality is, sometimes the truth is a little too accurate with the camera.

What is it about showers and ideas? I was shampooing my hair in the shower, when an idea came to me to do a group photography class with some of my private students. I thought it would be a good addition to their lessons, and fun at the same time. Learning how to pose in front of the lens is an important element for any professional dancer to learn, especially for those preparing their portfolios. So I got out of the shower, and decided to make a call to Pat Berrett and talk to him about my idea. He thought it sounded like an interesting project, so we set a date for the group photo shoot and so our journey began. For our location, one of my students knew the owners of Project Tibet in Santa Fe, who allowed us to be photographed with their gorgeous jewelry on site for the day.

Out of the blue, one day I was looking at my Kachina dolls and the theme of the photo shoot emerged. I thought it would be interesting to do eye make up like the Native Americans do for ceremonial dances. Feathers came next, adding to this unconventional mix of New Mexico flair. We finished off our theme with gypsy skirts, corsets and hip scarves. I knew it was quite the mix of cultures, but that is what New Mexico is all about. So the six of us started working towards creating a melting pot costume, mixed with bling, colored fabrics and a little whimsy thrown in for ambiance. By the time the big day had arrived, everyone had invested time and money in creating their own impression of New Mexico. There was a multitude of colors that represented our skies, sunsets, landscape and people. We were walking works of art with each individual canvas a masterpiece.

The day of the photo shoot, I awoke with a feeling of dread, almost like something wasn't quite right. Call it woman's intuition or a hunch, but I knew the photo shoot was going to have problems before I ever got out of bed. My make up started off the morning by looking like a combination of Frankenstein's bride and a 5 year olds rendition of a scary person. My make-up wouldn't work, no matter what I did. Add the feathers that I attached to my eyelashes, and there standing before me was my impression of a scary owl. By the time I was done, my face looked like it belonged on a Picasso painting. Where the hell was my professional belly dancer's face? She deserted me and obviously stayed under the covers!

One of my students was thirty minutes late, coming to my house which made me pace. By the time she arrived, I was ready to wash off my Picasso impersonation and dive back into bed. We adjusted costumes and make up problems, finally heading off to our photo shoot location, which was in an hours drive from Albuquerque. I noticed that my anxious feeling was coming back with a vengeance, but I squashed it like a bug and kept on driving, trying to focus on positive thoughts. As we approached Project Tibet's parking lot, I was awe struck at the exploding color coming off the girl's eclectic, gypsy costumes. New Mexico was alive and well with each and every one of them. We attracted curious onlookers, who gathered around and watched us prepare for our photo shoot.

As we all walked in together, I noticed that Pat was starting to set up for the indoor shots which gave us time to select our jewelry, readjust feathers, corsets and the occasional bindi glitch. Our first group shot was on large floor rugs, piled up two feet high with colorful walls and hand carved furniture. As Pat started to get prepared for his shots, I noticed that he didn't want me to position the girl's arms and legs. We had talked about this before we set the date, but for some reason unbeknownst to me he changed his mind, so I followed his direction. The problems started when a student to my right kept putting her hand in front of my face, which was starting to annoy me to no end. I would move her hand down and up it would go with each flash. I looked stressed and unfocused due to worry and slight irritation. I would do my best to help the girls and follow Pat's direction but some of the girl's came across like mannequins, with awkwardly positioned legs and stiff arms. It was their first photo shoot so it was natural for them to freeze in place out of fear or shyness. Looking back, I feel like that first group of photos was like herding cats for Pat. He had to deal with various conversations going on at once, nervous giggles and the occasional direction challenged student. I was really impressed that he was able to hold the photo shoot together.

With this experience, I learned that sometimes it's not always written in the stone for an idea to work out. The experience was rich in atmosphere, high energy and just plain fun so I felt we accomplished more than just modeling lessons, we gained a sense of group camaraderie that we didn't have before. At days end, we all took Pat out for a well deserved lunch surrounding him with our glorious female chatter.

A Work in Progress

I couldn't let it rest, because my photo shoot idea was bursting to come alive, once more. I thought we should change up the surroundings, keeping it in Albuquerque. With the changes I wanted to make, my friends Mike and Tish Miller came to mind. Mike was the photographer who had taken photographs of me at the Wild Spirit Wolf sanctuary along with his wife Tish, who is an artist with many talents including fine jewelry and print making. Mike found a wonderful warehouse, owned by independent film producer, Paul Porter of Rogue Taurus Productions. Mike is an independent film producer, owner of 9Point Productions himself, so the fact that he had an in with the film community was definitely a plus.

Unfortunately not all my students could make this photo shoot because of conflicting schedules, but the rest who could, worked on changing up costuming and prepared for another chance to be photographed. Mike also arranged for a make up artist to be on location the day of the shoot for a few hours which definitely helped with any makeup malfunctions. We were excited to model Tishes jewelry because each piece was one of a kind, with a presence to them that felt as if they were alive.

The morning of the photo shoot, I felt excited and relaxed. It started off without any make up glitches or delays. I was so relieved not to be impersonating any paintings or animals. We worked from 9:00 in the morning until 3:00 in the afternoon. Considering it was indoors for the duration of the photo shoot, we were able to experiment and create different scenarios to get different types of photos. I was able to position arms and legs as Mike took memorable shots.

The learning aspect of any photo shoot helps to create dancers who understand the camera. It's not always easy to be real in front of a camera. A pose has to be believable for the viewers just as much as it does for the artist. So my students learned that if they didn't believe in themselves, it would immediately come across that way onto the photograph, because the camera doesn't lie. They also learned that in creating good photographs, there is a lot of hard work that goes into making that happen.

Both photo shoots were hard work but in different ways. The first photo shoot with Pat was raw for most of them, so they had no emotion. They held positions that didn't work because they were holding them at awkward angles out of anxiety. They didn't know how to pose in a relaxed manner, so Pat had to coax them into positions as he was photographing them. In the second photo shoot with Mike, sometimes they held a position that was painful to the point of arms or legs going numb. With both photo shoots, they had to go within themselves to pull out the dancer hiding away that was too shy to come out.

At the end of the Santa Fe photo shoot everyone was tired from standing and anticipating each shot. Everyone was going on pure adrenalin so a sense of exhaustion could be felt throughout the group at days end. By the end of the second photo shoot with Mike, everyone was tired but they felt like they had learned how to finally relax. With both experiences under their belts I know my students learned how both photographers worked and connected with them. Both Pat and Mike have unique skills that have always added a bit of panache to any of the projects I have done with them. The important thing is to find the photographer that you not only can build a partnership with, but when you work together, it's pure magic. To say I'm lucky I found both Pat Berrett and Michael L. Miller is an understatement!

14 - Choreography- An Individual Journey

"Choreography is the best lineage women can leave for each other because the story within the dance says so much about each generation"

There is nothing more frustrating than learning a choreography that is not your own, and then having to dance to music as if you hear the movements, the way the dance instructor does. Music calls to us all, but how we answer her is the key element to our individual creativity. In saying this, I must admit that there are two sides to the choreography coin. If you don't familiarize yourself with both sides then you can become deaf to other peoples ideas and creativity. There is always something to learn from other dancer's creativity, but it is up to you to figure out what that lesson is. Sometimes through movement that is not our own, we understand how music stimulates and inspires other dancers.

Not only is this important, but it is necessary to understand various types of rhythm in ways that would otherwise be foreign to us. Rhythm is the part of choreography that tells us not only about the dancer but how she understands the connection between music and movement. Moving to music in ways that are not familiar to us, allows us to take off our own blinders that we create from dancing to our isolated beat.

What comes to mind, are the workshops that I have gone to, where I was the one dancer going left when everyone else was going right. In my beginning years, I wanted to be in the front of class, but I eventually ended up, slowly moving to the back, realizing that the dancers behind me didn't appreciate my two left feet. I found out to my dismay that the speed in which I was supposed to learn various choreographies was an impossible Olympian feat. I could never figure out why some of the dance teachers thought everyone can get their choreography down in a two hour time span. It left an imprint on my mind, which lead me down the line, to teach in a format combining various combinations women could put in their own choreographies. This made more sense to me and I know dancers are always looking for a new moves or combinations put together in a way they haven't thought of yet. The interesting thing here is how we move within our own bodies, according to how we understand choreography.

Questions regarding movement seem to be answered only when we start to do our own homework. Individual, interpretive studies regarding our own choreography, seems to come when we have a hands on approach within our dancing methodologies.

If you look at in the box choreography, you will find there are venues when this type of curriculum and study works to your advantage, especially if you are in a troupe. Also, in the box choreography works well if you are performing at a venue, where you get called at the last minute. But I have to say, spontaneous choreography works well here too, so the best thing to do is be proficient in both. Choreography is very important when it comes to the interpretation of the music; pauses, accents, posing, traveling steps and layering because all combined, make it come alive. Combinations can become robotic if you don't put life into them and I would have to state further, that technique can't help if movement isn't felt. A good choreographer understands that she is the visual interpreter from the music to the audience.

Restaurant dancing has been my refuge, where I had the creative freedom to dance uninhibited within the confines of intimate crowds. I feel a person has to have a certain amount of confidence, to be able to do spontaneous choreography, because it can feel so raw at times. Performing for over 15 years in restaurants, helped me improve on my nightclub and stage performing. I became more personable on stage because I learned to enjoy the audience with a genuine enthusiasm and confidence. As I found out, there are experiences where spontaneous choreography comes in handy, especially when you least expect it.

Case in point; I was dancing at a nightclub in Houston called, The Mirage. This particular night for some reason, a couple of the musicians started to argue in the middle of my show. I could hear them arguing over the music, and neither would let up. I felt like I was dancing to a broken record for what seemed an eternity. I turned around and yelled for them to stop arguing because I was about to melt off the stage. After my show, everything seemed fine between the musicians and as I tried to talk to them about what happened, they just looked at me like I was nuts.

I recall another time when I worked with a talented and wonderful band called the Arabic Band in Dallas, the drummer on one particular night was really grumpy. We ended up doing what felt like a 20 minute drum solo because he was mad at his girlfriend. As I lay on the floor of my dressing room, literally seeing stars, I realized spontaneous choreography literally saved me from a fate worse than death. Afterwards, I had a heart to heart talk with the drummer and told him to give me a heads up the next time they had a spat.

Remembering to be ourselves, and to implement our body language the way we speak words, sets us apart from each other. An audience can tell if a dancer doesn't believe in her dance within minutes of her performance. Believing in ourselves is really half the battle, because once we gain our confidence, we find those pieces of ourselves that emerge and come to life on stage. When a dancer shares with her audience, she brings to life her understanding of her interpretive dance. There has to be a comfort level with performing or the message becomes unclear. This means that whether a dancer does spontaneous or in the box choreography, the audience wants to see a confident performer.

I'll tell you all a little secret, in the box choreography has tripped me up more then I can say, but I think it has to do with my personality. For some bizarre reason, my body doesn't want to do the same choreography over and over again, even though gigs are different. I tend to naturally change moves around without thinking about it. Restaurant dancing could be the culprit, because there is so much that happens when you are performing with people moving around you. You have to have eyes in the back of your head, so my Mom wasn't joking when she said she had eyes in the back of her head. I must have inherited them from her!

Spontaneous choreography seems to be a better fit for me because I instinctively know how my combinations feel in my body. However I have always admired troupes who can do amazing choreography or solo performers that seem to be able to make their in the box choreography fresh each time they perform it. Since in the box choreography is based on uniform counting, it makes sense that it works for troupes because they can work within this structure and start from the ground up. But I have come to a place in my dance where odd counting for opposition hip combinations makes more sense to me. I look at my hips as twins but not identical twins. They each have their own personality which makes for a more interesting story telling. Again this is a way of thinking that has only come to me as I have gotten older. I think it's the same story for many dancers, who have been performing for many years; we crave change and become open to new possibilities that we previously would have been closed off to.

Spontaneous choreography in my view, allows the audiences enthusiasm to finish off dancers performances in a way that allows for a connection to happen naturally. When I work on spontaneous choreography, I consider it only 90 percent finished before I go on stage, because I enjoy inviting the audience to finish the last 10 percent with me. Depending on what kind of audience I have, it's amazing what can happen, since there is a unique blend of creative energy and excitement mixed together It feels like a mystical pact or bond I make with the audience that becomes apart of my creative process. This is the part of choreography that makes it all worth while, because sharing the joy of the dance can really change the audience's perception of not only a dancer's performance, but of her dance form as a whole.

In the box choreography reminds me of timed movements, that when put together become fluid and separately individual. Performers, who know their dance character, can pull out a performance that becomes a constant flow of movements that hide the obvious structured design. Fluidity makes all the difference here, because movement choreographed to the phrasing in music, has to have a purpose beyond what the audience expects. This means that with in the box choreography, the element of surprise has to be choreographed in.

I have to admit, that with all the dancers performing now, they are obviously bringing in modern and edgy influences that showcase distinctive views and tastes in their dance. Not everyone is inspired the same way, but sometimes in watching other dancers perform, you can see them reveal their true nature. The flavors of belly dance are numerous, and constantly changing like ice cream; we all have our favorite flavor but we add in variety as our tastes change. I have always thought dancers are like savory flavors, either a local favorite or an exotic twist. But attitudes added in like sprinkles, can change an ordinary dancer into something unexpected. Years ago, I watched a well known dancer perform on video and was taken aback at her personality on stage. She had a command of her audience and the bottom line was, they loved her. It mystified me because while her dancing was memorable and well executed, it wasn't particularly my favorite style. But I have to say, watching her perform on stage, reminded me of a Queen holding a trance over her viewers, because she saw the audience as her court. That was a lesson I'll never forget, because her attitude, along with her choreography made the difference. I realized technique is only half the battle in choreography. Choreography isn't only about believing in yourself, it's also about defining a creative expression that can only be given by you, through your interpretation of your own design. You have to be the artist of your own design, sculpture or art form, besides being the saleswoman of what you create from one performance to the next. The hardest part about choreography, is selling our interpretation of our dance not only to the masses but to our community. The point is, there has to be a sold sign upfront before we ever get on stage. This sets the professionals apart from the amateurs.

Is choreography all in the mind? The crutch of in the box choreography is keeping the moves only in the head. Eventually we all have to rely on feeling a move and knowing it is done correctly. This means you have to have a trust within yourself that comes with a maturity level that not only survives life's hard knocks, but brings about an overwhelming reprieve from our inner Goddess.

As a choreographer, I feel the best lessons we can learn are the kind that leave us scratching our heads. If all performances went as planned, we wouldn't learn the pitfalls of goofing up or that elated feeling of succeeding. I have watched videos of my performances, where I didn't follow through with my own rules of thumb and ended up looking like a sad parody of myself. I must admit, I am guilty along with many professional dancers who work on their performances a couple of days before a show. My inclusion here is I am able to do this now, after performing twenty years in dance. I thought about it and wondered if it's a lackadaisical way of doing things, or a sign of the times? Has this change affected the quality and sustainability of the dance form itself? How different are we from dancers twenty or thirty years ago? Styles have changed along with the times, so with the modern woman dancing today, it seems logical that the methodology of practicing and preparing for a show follows suit especially for the professional, on the go dancers.

Choreography itself is different now, but the reasons aren't just different generations coming in but a multitude of agendas getting mixed into how this dance form is taught today. Students are implementing what they learn from their teachers and YouTube videos. A students dance image isn't as easily molded like years past, the media attraction along with the fly by night desire to get new moves asap, is apart of our world now. But work, motherhood and home dynamics have made a few teachers examples of the, do as I say, not as I do genre, which makes practicing ethics go out the window. I experienced this when I was dancing three or four nights in a row, the last thing I wanted to do was practice on my days off.

Life dictates to us what needs to be addressed, but it's easy to push aside what is immediately in front of us. In the end, my ability to do tighter choreographies was undermined by my need to just get my performance over with so I could get to my next gig. I thought this was where spontaneous choreography would come in and save the day, but by letting my practice ethics go out the window, my spontaneous choreography became sloppy and uninspiring. So the bottom line is that no matter what kind of choreography you do, you have to practice…period.

"Sometimes dancers are born molded and nurtured in the arts becoming the living essence of what they represent" Leyla Najma

Since we are all apart of the YouTube generation, it's obvious the mass amount of belly dance videos up now is astounding. Students and dancers can actually see a large number of moves performed, gaining ideas otherwise not available to them. But with this type of technology available, I feel we have lost some of our instincts to go within ourselves, pulling out those individual and unique moves. When I do my online instructional videos, it doesn't occur to me to go look at other videos for ideas. I'm too busy trying to figure out how to implement what inspires me into an easy and understandable video. I have a plethora of combinations inside me that exist from living life on the stage. The world is my inspiration and when she envelopes me, choreographies spill out of me; a telltale sign of an impassioned dancer. This is a sign for many of us, the markings of a belly dancer who composes her dance to a tune only she can hear.

But with our modern belly dance communities, a thought crossed my mind, are dancers becoming blind to their own inspired creativity? Maybe today's fast food generation feels a need to acquire moves at the drop of a hat because the pace of belly dance has changed along with her direction. Visually to me, creativity borrowed in this fashion always looks unoriginal.

My view regarding dance videos has made creating videos for dancers harder, because in the end it's not like I don't realize this is my business. But what I always hope to do with my videos is to inspire dancers to change things up and create their own interpretation of what they have just learned. Perhaps this is what we do when we see moves that inspire us anyways. My philosophy is based on helping women understand the need to learn the basics of dance, but at the same time they have to figure out how to absorb the information. How a woman absorbs dance into her body is the first signature or mark of the dancer within. A dancer has to be able to put moves and combinations together whether she is doing in the box or out of the box choreography that is original and natural to her. This means that choreography has to have something original from the dancer that says this is my statement to the world. Borrowed choreography is somebody else's statement and usually most dancers unless they are in a troupe, won't understand the original meaning.

I'm going to opine here a little in regards to class curriculum. An interesting result that happens with choreography is what I call, the critic characteristic. Once choreography has blossomed in a dancer and her path is flooded with creative ideas, she can develop a choreography censor personality that begrudges anyone else's creative expression. We may all have this peculiar personality in us to varying degrees, only because as I said before, we all hear music differently. This altered personality, can cause problems, because the bottom line with some dancers is competitive rivalry.

Years ago, before I had my own studio, I rented space at various dance studios. I had a dance acquaintance who I rented from twice a week and this worked well enough for awhile. As a working dancer, I would occasionally get dance gigs during class days so on one of these occasions, I asked my dance friend to cover one of my classes for me. The following week I noticed I had a lot of no shows and was informed by some of my students that my dance friend led them to believe that I wasn't an experienced teacher. A few believed her and left my class. With my dance acquaintances unscrupulous behavior a problem, I realized there was no safety net with her. Someone like that has no scruples or community morals. But I have to say, the end result ultimately was a good one, because it pushed me into getting my own studio.

When a teacher is working with students on choreography or combinations, the process needs to be unhindered so that concepts can start taking shape. How can someone who has no clue regarding the class curriculum, come in and comment on its content? Two words, choreography critic.

It's important to get across how important it is to have ethics and camaraderie in this dance form. When students are ready to create their own choreographies, they also need to understand how essential it is to mix in a little humility to stay grounded. In the end, there will be things you like about other peoples dancing and things you won't. If all a dancer can do is mouth off, then she creates a mood where negativity spreads like a virus. This is where the clicks come in and the community gets broken up into isolated factions. It won't matter what type of choreography a dancer creates, she won't be appreciated in her own back yard.

Ultimately, our choreography has to mean something besides just movements to music. Martha Graham stated that, dance is the hidden language of the soul and body, so dancers who pull their choreography from inside themselves reach for this sacred ground. Others who are looking for a quick fix, will ultimately burn out and continually search for more moves without realizing that the test for all choreographers, is the original masterpiece of their own creativity.

In the box or out of the box choreography psychologically liberates dancers from their own self imposed consequences of blame, guilt or shame. There is a freedom, moving to music in a way that is all your own. We can rise above this earthly plain and experience life; existing for no other reason, consumed with this elixir of dance, which we all drink to excess. Instead of stumbling around like drunken fools, we embody the synchronicity of creativity and we allow it to move within our bodies in a way that is food for our souls. Choreography is a way to understand our own meaning of who we are, and it is a tool we can use to define our own identity; the one thing we either alienate ourselves from through out life or we become indifferent strangers to. It's like going in and seeing the inner child, talking with her the way she needs to be talked to in order to heal and then move on.

Choreography is my meditation, my fix, my release and finally my rebirth. With choreography we are constantly being given back pieces of ourselves, so we can complete the puzzle of our lives. Sometimes the blank spots are comforting. I often wonder, if I finally get all the pieces in place what would be left to choreograph. Sometimes it's in the sorrow, pain and suffering of life that we create our best work. But then choreography teaches us that balance, harmony and synergy are life's foundations, the natural way of creating. For me choreography is all of the above and more.

It seems for each mountain climbed or in this instance choreographed; there is another mountain in the distant horizon, calling to us that is foreboding and intimidating. It is for this reason, why I am a choreographer. The mountain becomes a goal of unknown origins that await me. I tend to stumble along learning how to sculpt and mold my dance into a story worth telling. I hope at the same time, to find another puzzle piece to complete who I am. It's a calling that not everyone answers to, but those of us who do; we get to experience a rite of passage that changes us forever.

Choreography is the best lineage women can leave for each other, because the story within the dance says so much about each generation. In the end of my search for what choreography is all about, I have come to understand that it is about educating, supporting and inspiring women to define movement in their own individual way so that this dance will survive. It is about standing up for who we are as women and not apologizing for our creativity. It's a blessed way of leaving apart of ourselves to the world, so we won't be forgotten. In essence, choreography is about healing and becoming the sculpted masterpiece of which we are in the flesh…yes we become our own masterpiece!

15 - Borrowing or Stealing Moves

"If we dance our creativity everyday, the artist in us will always have a muse."

The Borrower

Years ago when I was in Egypt, I was watching TV and was overjoyed to see belly dancing on many of the channels. As I settled down and started watching Nagua Fuad perform one of her amazing choreographies, I could have sworn I had seen it performed somewhere or something similar. I couldn't put my finger on it, so I kept on watching her dance and than bingo; I remembered where I had seen it. The performance Nagua Fuad had performed was from around the late 60's or early 70's, and a performance that looked similar to hers was done by a dancer in the later part of the 80's. Since I was in my early stages of learning belly dance, I didn't know if it was ok to borrow choreography from a well known dancer. Some of the moves were different, but the essence of the dance was definitely from Nagua Fuad. It made me wonder about choreography, and how our dance is actually passed down from one dancer to another. Taking it a few steps further, I wondered about themes in dance, curriculum terminology, and styles. With so many dancers in our community, how can we actually know if moves are original or taken from another dancer? Does it matter?

As I found out talking to friends, it became a definite cut and dry topic, because in the end, it does matter. Another quandary tossed around was copyrighting curriculums and choreography. Is this ethical or even reasonable in our dance field since so many moves are based upon the same foundation terminology? It may sound funny or strange to think of copy righting choreography or a curriculum, but as I progressed in my dance, I saw what can happen when people take your verbiage, combinations and moves without giving due credit.

It's evident that choreography taught in classes and workshops, attracts students who want to ride on the belly dance wave of success. With some students, teachers have to be careful because short cuts are the name of game for a specific few. There are always students who want to see the view from the top before their time. It's an obvious human desire to want to look into a crystal ball, perhaps to maneuver ones career a bit easier, but life teaches us that it's not always about the end goal that matters. Short cuts can take away from the experience of working towards ones goals, taking away the fortitude and appreciation on how a person got there in the first place. A faulty foundation created by short cuts can crack without warning, leaving an unsuspecting dancer vulnerable. Becoming ignorant of how cracks happen is a result that stems from not taking the time to find out where the faulty ledges are. Failure and success can become synonymous with a dancers point of reference, especially when she is blinded by what she thinks she will find when she reaches the top. There are always illusions based on our imagination versus the truth.

With student enthusiasm in mind, I realized with so many workshops happening and so many wonderful dancers teaching their choreography, copyrighting moves is just about as impossible as it is impractical. It would be futile because there is no way a dancer could say a move is hers, unless she is famous for her own style and technique. But realistically, fame doesn't always shield dancers from choreography thieves.

What about the wonderful dancers that are not as well known who teach their choreography locally at workshops? This seems to be where the short cut wannabes come in, silently waiting. Moves and choreography can be performed in restaurants and shows out of state without anyone knowing the better. So my question is, should we as dancers share the wealth of information and tell others our secrets or keep our secrets to ourselves? Is our dance really completely ours or do we share in the divine inspiration that allows anyone to enter?

The Carbon Copy Complex

It's logical to assume that most dancers go to workshops or take classes locally for the choreography. A type of problem that can spiral out of control is, if another dancer takes information taught in a workshop or class and starts to teach it as her own with no credit given to the original teacher. I have wondered is this stealing or is it the way it's always been? This led me to another question regarding "borrowing" another dancer's style of eloquence. If a dancer is not well known, her manner of speaking along with her dance technique can be taught and her identity as a dancer imitated with no one the wiser. The responsibility lies within each dancer and her duty to give credit where credit is due. There are two types of dancers; those who want all the glory for themselves or those who are willing to share the glory. You just have to figure out which one you are.

I have friends who have taught classes for years and they have their own method they created throughout their years of trial and error. To understand this right of passage, takes years of training and living dance but unfortunately for younger dancers this is a hard lesson for them to understand. This right of passage is the best way to teach from because there is no need to lie; experience says it all. You can give your students an established choreography lineage besides the recollection of performing it. This skill cannot be borrowed because the authenticity would only be a weak imitation of the original. So how can anyone teach another person's curriculum without giving them credit? They are already at a disadvantage because experience is the well that all teachers draw from. The well of knowledge overflows for those who drink from her depths of creativity. To take from this well you have to give something back that equals what you take. This is the way the *divine source energy* keeps flowing for all who use her.

The Double Up

A couple of years ago, I went to a dance festival that a friend of mine had been putting on for quite a few years. At about the same time of year, another studio decided to have their workshop and show on or about the same time. I'm not the sharpest knife in the drawer, but I do remember my friend having her yearly workshops at a particular time of year based on her theme. Selective memory served its purpose, because the other studio decided that date was theirs. Justifications come in all shapes and sizes but this seriously didn't make any sense. My dance friend's festival coincides with a historical celebration that takes place on a specific time of year.

I call this problem the "double up" because I have heard stories about this happening and I can't quite figure out why. Do you know how many days there are in a year? Does mass hypnosis take over with dates subliminally being placed in peoples brains? Think about it, it is harder to double up than change a date. It seems inconsiderate not to check and see if there's another workshop happening on a particular weekend. Scheduled dates should be respected and honored because it's like stealing money from your own community. For some dancers this is a business and livelihood, yes competitive but since when are we like *Corporate America*?

Your Theme is my Theme

Have you ever had an idea for a show and mentioned it to another dancer, who before you knew it, put on a show with your idea? I had this done to me years ago and realized I just plain and simple had a big mouth. I wonder to this day about the dancer who ran with my idea, what was her responsibility to me if any? When I questioned her on it, she rationalized by stating that I hadn't done anything with it, so she didn't think I would mind. I just looked at her with a blank look on my face because I couldn't believe I allowed her to steal my idea, right out from under me.

I was actually in the works, getting things together for my show but instead of going head with my plans, I backed down like a spineless wimp. The irony here was, the fact she asked me to perform in her show which was my idea. To this day, I can't remember if I did or didn't dance in the show. I think I blocked it out of my mind because I was embarrassed that I didn't stand up for myself. Today if somebody did this to me, my Hyde persona would come out and they wouldn't know what hit them.

When it comes to productions and shows, it is so important to respect the themes and ideas that dancers come up with. If you know what a theme of a show is ahead of time, respect the time line before you do something similar.

The Age of Videos and Karma

Today's technology has helped created the age of instructional and performance videos. Most dancers find it easier to purchase them and view them in the comfort of their own living rooms. We can also view old videos of famous dancers, absorbing into our genres a variety of styles and techniques. So the question, can a dancer of today say that a specific move is hers, depends on how long she has been dancing and what her style is all about. Style can't be imitated or borrowed it has to come from within a dancer who understands her own body and divine inspiration.

This will be a debatable topic of discussion for years to come, because of the taboos regarding learning from home. Some dancers and teachers don't understand that the needs of women are changing along with everything else. I have many instructional videos out now, so at this point I feel that instructional videos are a way to share, educate and nurture as many women as possible. The only downfall with instructional videos is the propensity for some dancers to plagiarizing advertizing ideas, running with marketing verbiage, technical ideas and strategies.

If there is anything I learned during my apprenticing years with medicine men and women, it's the Universes indifference to the laws of karma. Even with this indifference, the Universe is constantly watching what we do and there is a lesson to learn in every word or deed that is spoken or done to another. The lesson itself is usually based on the power of a person's intention, positive or negative. So I wonder how people who copy another's creativity think they are immune to their own actions. Negative actions and words usually come back, reminding us of our indiscretions, in ways that humble us through Karma, ten fold.

Borrowing Curriculum

Sometimes at the end of the day our curriculum is our loyal companion that stays with us until we close the doors. A dancer's curriculum can be like sacred transcripts of a life's journey that is the key element into keeping the studio doors open for business.

The question is how much of a teacher's curriculum is hers? There are fundamental aspects of this dance that have been taught through out the history of this dance. The key difference from basic generic text is the dancer's journey and the understanding she has for her craft. One problem that affects teachers indiscriminately is students who are willing to take their curriculum and claim it as theirs. What this means is students bring into the studio the rudimentary elements of everything they either have or lack in life. If a student's lifestyle is dysfunctional we end up dealing with the side effects that trickle down and materialize into various problems in the studio. An experienced dancer understands that even if her curriculum is taken, the training and experiences that made her curriculum what it is can't be taken. The best part of being the creator of an individual curriculum is the original design or signature makes it obvious who it belongs to. It takes more then just talk to teach a curriculum, you have to understand the esthetics of a dance form by personally studying it's roots and history. Movement can be a flat inconsequential extension of limited understanding or a poetic gesture that speaks volumes to the soul.

A Combination of Many

When it's all said and done, belly dance is not just a community dance, it is a collective consciousness that floods the senses and possesses the heart and soul of all dancers. In a way we are all combinations of many teachers and dancers who have influenced our careers. So when we learn a move and perform it, we keep it alive. I guess what I'm getting at is, when a seasoned dancer has nothing to prove in her dance but to dance for the pure joy of it, she than becomes the essence of her dance. This can't be copied or borrowed because the essence of each dancer's spirit is unique unto herself. If each dancer keeps her dance a definition of who she is, than she won't feel the need to take what is not hers or she will be mature enough to give credit where credit is due. Besides, there is too much original creativity out there to be mimicking other dancers or their styles. My motto is, *"Creativity is not defined but lived."* I keep this in mind so that every time I create my own choreographies, I am true to my own inspiration.

16 - YouTubing Myself Under the Covers

"There's nothing like succeeding on stage and then again there are always those reminders that we are mortal after all. A twist of the ankle, a fumble with a veil or a costume mishap is our calling card along with a video camera recording our unfortunate deeds."

One morning I got up from bed, sleepily went over to my computer to check to see if I had any emails, and there in front of me was an email saying, I have a "comment" on one of my videos on You tube. My heart skipped a beat, and my eyes went cross-eyed for a minute, okay…mostly because I had just woken up, but it was still traumatic. So what did I do, you guessed it, I jumped back into bed under the covers! I never used to mind "comments," but for some bizarre reason viewers think they can write just about anything, which includes negative, rude and insulting comments. In the beginning, I put my videos up because I was proud of them, and wanted to share them with other belly dance enthusiasts. But within months, it became clear that my videos were targets for just about every comment under the sun. My whole attitude gradually changed from wanting to share my videos with the masses, to hiding in the bushes thanks to the computer trolls. So I decided it was time to stay out of the bushes and take a good look at this strange phenomenon I call, *computer trolling*.

It was obvious that my problem seemed to be the habitual response to computer trolls, ambushing me. I realized people don't have to have manners when they hide behind a computer, and they can pass on negativity without any forethought, because watching videos isn't equivalent to talking to a person, it's an opinion game. It's almost like technology has zapped the intellectual capacity for verbal compassion and traded it for an indifference that gradually metamorphosis's into a troll mentality. Being an entertainer takes more back bone than a regular job, but in some ways it intensifies our inhibitions and fears. The more a dancer invests in her dancing, the greater the chances she has at achieving her goals. But put together an insensitive person, hiding behind technology, and you have a nemesis bent on opposing any dancer's accomplishments. To put it bluntly to be the target of negativity sucks!

We all have preferences in life and dance, but this penchant doesn't give anyone the go ahead to oppress others creative efforts. If you dance, than you know what it takes to get on stage and perform in front of an audience. So our common diversity is the fact that, whether we dance Egyptian, Tribal or Fusion, we all risk the same vulnerability by placing our videos on the internet. Videotaping performances is a great way for dancers to see themselves, the way the audience does. It's a great learning tool. So then, why would anyone want to put down our human right to be creative, for the sole purpose of being spiteful? I wondered this exact same thing, as I finally crept out of bed and decided to face my "comment". With a foreboding feeling, I typed in my password and took a deep breath and started to read the comment. With a huge sigh of relief, I quietly said a big thank you to the universe, because it was a nice comment. Within seconds, I could breathe normal and the tense feeling I had left me. As I sat back in my chair, I realized that I could avoid all of this by just taking my videos down. It seemed simple enough, but it didn't feel right. Taking them down seemed like the coward's way out, so I realized that if I wanted to change the rules of the game, I had to stay in it.

Before putting my videos up on various sites, I wasn't so mistrustful and only hid under the covers watching scary movies. But I had no clue how clueless some people could be, when it comes down to just plain manners. Our internet culture seems to be going into an insensitive state of mind that is spreading like a virus. I realized, not everybody uses tact behind the computer plus some don't have any to begin with. Something else I find crazy, is people who aren't even dancers, becoming critics on a dance form they know nothing about. They are the ones who seem to be the most consistent, throwing opinion darts at anyone who counters their views. There is no greater waste of time, then feeling the need to defend the right to create and choreograph dance. Every dancer who is inspired by the divine knows that to be in direct contact with such inspiration, is the root desire and purpose of their artistry. This is a main reason why I feel so many women love belly dance, because the end results of their efforts are showcased in a way that frames and enhances all their senses.

Unfortunately, there is a dark side we occasionally experience through out our careers. The metamorphosis that takes place with some women who become dancers, perplexes me, because they develop scathing opinions on just about everything in this dance form. I think viewpoints are valid and necessary in life, but we have to look at the "hen pecked" mentality that's associated towards women. It's obvious the pop culture of today wants to be informed, directed and encouraged but the tactlessness of some in this group, can affect their need to devalue the very thing in which they themselves want to be accepted in.

In today's society, we have to beware of creating and perpetuating an environment that embraces the "hen pecked" hierarchy, even in the confines of a computer.

The Universe is constantly listening to what we say, and there is a lesson to learn in every word that is spoken. The lesson itself is usually based on the power and intention of a person's words. So I wonder how people, who degrade and diminish other's creativity, can then think that they are immune to their own impertinent words. As entertainers, we have to take to heart the emotional and compassionate aspects of being human, since we represent all aspects of humanity on stage.

Probably the groups that puzzle me the most are dancers who make comments that give the connotation that they can dance better than anyone up on YouTube. So okay, I ask, where are their videos? They never seem to have any videos up, and if you ask to see one of their performances, the communication stops. The bottom line is, if a dancer wants to leave a negative comment, than she needs to put up a performance of herself to show that she can actually even dance. But it's easy, to hide behind a comment and to become an anonymous critic. One of my philosophical ways of looking at these kinds of people is that they will eventually end up looking like their comments through time. So if you look around you, they are easy to spot, because they are the end result of their opinions and attitudes. Negativity is the dress that shows off all the imperfections and magnifies them with no regard or consideration for the wearer. Pretty much it's just an ugly dress!

But I have to say the comments that really bug the hell out of me, are what I call, "beyond pointless". I have many instructional videos out and for one specific video that my husband put a trailer up on various sites including a yahoo video group. In the trailer, I talk about the contents of my video and why I produced it. Low and behold, I had a dancer comment that because there was no demonstration included, I must not be any good. Another said I was just talking about myself, so there was nothing there. I guess what she was trying to tell everyone was that I was boring. So how did the one dancer come up with the assumption that I'm not any good? My only guess is through ESP...not! As for the other comment, unbeknownst to this woman, most people won't spend money making a video about nothing. So the comments were supposed to warn viewers of what? After thinking about it, I realized these people are in everyday life, so why wouldn't they show their small minded selves here? Realistically, if I wanted to be immune from critics, than I picked the wrong dance form to get into. It just goes with the territory, whether you perform publically or put a video up on YouTube.

Maybe, I'm being a little too sensitive here but let's face it, when people hide behind their computers they morph into their Dr. Hide personas. They write comments they wouldn't say in public without getting into a fight. Actually, we do have Reality TV, so this point is a bit mute now. There have been a few occasions where I observed groups of dancers, watching performances, emphatically whispering comments to each other, yet thankfully not yelling their opinions up to the stage. Most dancers tend to have some form of tact when they go to shows. I feel the same should be said for watching videos. If you don't like how a dancer is performing, than don't watch the video. It's that simple or is it?

I decided for curiosities sake, to check out other videos to see if anybody else was going through what I was. As I read some of the comments published, I was totally shocked. I realized, I was in good company. On one video in particular, people were questioning if the dancer was really a woman. Her talent was overshadowed by an on going discussion that had nothing to do with her dance ability. Is this what our community really wants for our dance? I have to admit, I was lured in by the comments which took precedence over the dancer's ability to perform. This twisted mindset placed our beautiful dance form into a murky place of inconsequence and slight perversion. I also became part of the problem because for those few brief moments, I sold out for what ultimately tore down the dancer's right to perform. Yes, it's that easy to get sucked in.

So it donned on me that if this is the direction our society is going, it's no wonder we are dealing with people who are desensitized to their own humanity. When we think with a computer, we become detached from our community. We don't react as a single minded person, but as a result of a technology matrix. This can also effect our creative expression, especially with people who don't care if they affect us with their negative comments. I found the reason why the comments became so interesting was because my mental state became numb. Our humanity is what makes us different and unique as a species. We have technology that makes our lives better but in some ways, maybe it's making us forget our humanity. People want to be entertained at all costs, but as dancers are we willing to pay the price? Where will our dance be in ten years, and what kind of comments will we face with more Internet surfing on the rise? If we can't show humility within our own community, are we setting ourselves up for a mindless state of existence?

Our future rests on the shoulders of dancers who understand their dance and know why they are dancing. It shouldn't matter what other people say, but in our world maybe those "other" people are dancers. So as each of you view clips of videos, visualize yourself up there for the entire world to see. What would you do if someone said something unkind about your dance? It's important to remember that change starts with us, first. If we don't want our world changed into a dichotomy that makes no sense, than we need to focus on what's important. Just because someone isn't dancing your way, doesn't make them wrong. We need to be tolerant of each other, because this leads to a world that not only respects creative expression, but allows everyone to live and create their own expression of art. So in the end of my video surfing, I realized that we need to be able to express our opinions but how we do this says a lot about what kind of people we are. My focus is directed on my dance expression, not on what's wrong with somebody else's performance. This is why I still make videos today, and why I stand up for my creative right to produce videos, that make me happy. If I support my own creative right to dance, then maybe by example I will encourage other dancers to stand by their own creative rights, creating videos that mean something to them.

Since so many of us are belly dancers for life, I think we need to figure out how to be our own unique representation of our dance without comparing, demeaning or insulting anybody else's expression. The *Divine Unrest* comes from searching for our own testament, that keeps us traveling onward ceaselessly, looking for our inspiration. We hear, speak and move according to how we discover life and live it. So the motto, "*live and let live*," means more to us as a dance community. It means, we are tolerant of each others self expression and as we pass on the torch of humility and compassion, we inadvertently strengthen our communities foundation as a whole.

If there are times when I forget and start to feel sorry for myself, I look back to this one quote from a very dynamic woman who keeps me marching and continuously searching for my own tune and creative inspiration:

"There is vitality, a life force, a quickening that is translated through you into action, and since there is only one of you in all time, this expression is unique, and if you block it, it will never exist through any other medium and be lost. The world will not have it. It is not your business to determine how good it is, not how it compares with other expressions. It is your business to keep it yours clearly and directly, to keep the channel open. You do not even have to believe in yourself or your work. You have to keep open and aware directly to the urges that motivate you. Keep the channel open. No artist is pleased. There is no satisfaction whatever at any time. There is a queer, divine dissatisfaction, a blessed unrest that keeps us marching and makes us more alive than the others".

Martha Graham

17 - The Certification Question

"Life speaks to dancers, specifically in music and how we dance to her says so much about how we hear her."

This topic will either get me in hot water or a slight reprieve, based on how you feel about certifications. I am going to speak from the heart here, and probably step on a few toes, but know this is unintentional. My view of this dance form is based on my belief that belly dance is connected to the divine which transcends certifications. It would be like placing how someone lives life, on a score card and then judging how well they did. To me, belly dance is a feeling that we carry inside us that is like a sacred mark of the feminine divine. This passionate reaction to belly dance is what makes it so different from other dance forms, and why I feel it should not be in the certification arena.

I know what some of you (or many) may be thinking, we need this. One problem this will resolve is the bare minimal dancers out in our midst's, who are teaching from little or no training and experience. Adding to this, is the lack of consideration for cultural esthetics or historic aspects to belly dance, that is essential for a student's education. Unfortunately for students, there are dancers out in our world teaching from an inadvertence of these important and basic belly dance elements. The worst part for students is the fact they may not even know there is a difference between an experienced teacher or a novice one, until it's too late. Issues can escalate, causing beginner dancers to leave the dance with a bad taste in their mouths. The bare minimum dancer can try to get away with assuming the teacher role for only so long. Eventually cracks start to form because a dancer's foundation she builds along the way, strengthens by her experience and convictions. But in saying this, I think teachers and main core dancers can help by creating a tie with their own communities, creating a word of mouth that grapevines itself, hopefully keeping these types of individuals at bay.

With this dance form constantly changing and evolving with different styles, the certifications are questionable at best, because who is to say which new fusion styles are as legit as the original old school styles? With the constant changes, come different ideas and distinctive views on what a dancer feels is imperative to her learning. I don't want to necessarily learn Gothic belly dance, but I am sure there are many dancers who do and see Gothic belly dance as significant as Egyptian Cabaret. The basic foundation movements may be the similar, but the obvious changes in combinations along with modern and edgy ideals make this fusion style look like a distant cousin to old school belly dance. My point is, belly dance is constantly evolving, changing with each emerging generation, which is why it is such a different and distinctive dance form, so how do we certify the vast styles popping up with each generation?

As an older dancer, these questions matter to me because I have watched performances on stage that were foreign to me, yet I knew I was watching a genre of belly dance. I could see bits of foundation movements in the choreography, but they seemed to be pushed back into second act role. It's not a question of any specific dance style being wrong, it's just different and something I have to get used to. With these changes, the certification fever is rising in our midst and because of this fact there are a variety of women who are certifying their dance styles now. I say style of dance because I truly believe that this dance form is a very personal journey, and everyone has their story to share.

When we learn to dance it's really about learning how to embrace creativity within our bodies, and how to understand body awareness in movement. We have to be able to grasp movement in our bodies and understand how we move first, before we can understand the concept of a teacher's curriculum. As dancers, we become aware of our own interpretation of dance when we perform on stage but I wonder if we are aware that we are apart of the new revolution of change. Life evolves and so does dance.

The universe is so infinite and full of unknown galaxies that we can't see, yet we know they are there. You could no more contain the universe in a box then you could our dance form. There is so much of a person's own creativity to be discovered, that to me the pursuit of this desire is a constant for each dancer. So this brings to mind a question. Why would you want to be certified in an art form that has to do with the creative mind which is vast and full of new and boundless discoveries?

It's a known fact that if a dancer is learning a cultural dance form from a specific country, than she should learn to dance it correctly. But isn't learning different ways to dance like exploring new philosophies or educating the senses? Every time I learn something new, I feel as if I've traveled into the vast unknown. It's amazing how learning different cultural dances, changes us by enhancing our creative desires to emulate each subtle tradition and custom. So respect has to be a basic fundamental that needs to be embedded into every students learning process. Short cuts will only showcase a dancer's ignorance and indifference to her own art form. You can't hide inexperience from an audience full of dancers, especially if they know you are a teacher.

This is why belly dance reminds me of homeschooling, because it's an open book that not only allows each one of us to write in our stories, but we can rewrite the outcome by proxy as our skills are elevated. Traveling, meeting people and learning different cultural backgrounds is the best way to experience this dance form. This almost reminds me of keeping a diary, memoirs of not only the experience but feeling those emotional highs and devastating lows. Either way, it represents the school of life.

So I'm going to play devils advocate here; with so many dance teachers out in the world, how does any one person know if they are learning belly dance correctly or at least a way to progress in their dance?

To me, a certification usually represents a study or extended tutelage of something that means you're comparable to a graduate. Workshops aren't a stopping point in the learning process but apart a life time of study. There is so much to learn and discover that we instinctively become the eternal students of our dance. The climb to success never stops where we think it does, especially when there are so many varieties of subject matter to learn from. Belly dance has a way of playing tricks on the eyes because following one methodology can lead to something entirely different, so the illusion is thinking belly dance is a one way street. The lessons are endless and as we continue with our journeys, it's obvious within time that it's never how we imagined it to be in the first place. Thank goodness for those dancers who have put up markers for the rest of us!

We are very blessed to have generational dancers teaching, who professional dancers aspire to emulate and follow. These dancers have made our dance form respectable and popular and they have paved the way for dancers to follow in their footsteps. But with so many of these dancers teaching today, does this mean that you have to be certified by every one of these dancers? Everybody has their favorite dance teachers but what if you have multiple teachers that you really like, would you get certified with each teacher and if so how would you put the various curriculums together? Would you teach each one separately? How would you combine what you are certified in so that each curriculum stands on its own? If you combined curriculums would they mind? The answer is anybodies guess and I am sure if anyone does answer, the answers will vary.

There are many dancers in our field who want the certifications to show that they excel in their dance form, and I can understand this. The problems that arise from the certifications will depend on how many dancers offer them. But maybe I'm out to lunch here when I say problem, because as I said before, the certifications might end the problem we have with dancers coming in with little experience, competing for work and potential students. So the certifications seemingly might solve one problem, but they may create a new one unintentionally, especially for dance teachers like myself who don't offer certifications.

I don't give my student's certifications, but what they do get is a dance coach, one who will make sure they find their way of interpreting belly dance along with the proper training and skills necessary to succeed. I think it's important to travel along with students on their path, to answer questions and help them understand where their dance comes from. I don't want to teach my way of dance to such a point that students forget to find their own way in dance. It's important to help students feel success within themselves, so they know their creativity is indefinable. Since there is no end to self discovery, there is no end to the opportunities that come our way once we understand that our dance represents how we live life. My life says I'm just a dancer nothing more, nothing less.

I've been thinking about my studio years, and realized I gave out certificates to students who where ready to graduate to the next level. I required at least one year of study with me, before I tested any of my students. If they were ready to move up and showed progress, then it was inevitable that they would pass. Some of you could argue that I participated in the certification arena, and maybe I did to a certain degree. I think within a studio system this works, because the level certifications are based on a studio based curriculum and fundamentals that are intrinsic to every students learning process. The difference is that my certification didn't state they could go out in the world and teach belly dance. Maybe the certifications will start a new fad with today's generation of dancers, but as history has always shown us, it repeats itself and new problems arise to replace old ones. At this point, certifications are a coin toss and I'm just waiting to see how the changes play out.

But there is one aspect to the certifications that is unclear to me; if you have a veteran of this dance take a certification class along with a novice of a couple of years, where does that place them in the scheme of things? Is the novice able to go out, compete with the veteran and teach what she has just learned? With certifications, everyone has to complete the course to get certified. You might go, *duh* Leyla but not so fast. I know the instruction from the certification will pretty much be solid, but will the novice be able to take what she's learned and implement it in a way that makes sense down the line? I think we have to be realistic here. How can anyone stop a novice from teaching what she has become certified in? There is constant change happening with belly dance, ranging from all métiers of inspiration that dancer's pull from.

Experience is the tool that most veterans have up their sleeves, so this might be the dividing factor for implementing information. Experience showcases a veteran's tutelage in this dance form, or in other words her knowledge is understood by the brain, implemented into the body and expressed through emotion that is transformed into art. A dancer's individual expression by itself speaks volumes which is why the veteran dancer can say so much with just a glance, sway or gesture of the hand. Certifications can teach the technique but emotions have to be lived, breathed and experienced to complete a performance and make it powerful.

On the other hand, I have actually come across teacher's who are creating a new belly dance recipe for dancers, specifically those who want belly dance training yesterday with years of experience guaranteed. I have seen marketing schemes conjured up on the basis of certifications, offering dancers a life time of dance within a month. As a result, they are taking the integrity out of an ancient art form that has existed for thousands of years. The certifications can become a cross to bear for dancers like myself, who are dealing with students who have been certified by scammers trying to make a quick buck. Teaching dance is an art, and anybody who says otherwise doesn't understand this dance as art. So this can become a problem that can push a dance community's pot to boil over with unfair expectations. How can someone dance what they haven't learned, understood or felt?

I must confess that I am a free spirit and prefer to keep dance a life time endeavor that is my own vision quest. So for me, I would rather see life performed on stage that is a visual piece of art in progress. Are any of us truly satisfied with our dance or are we continually searching for the perfect move, choreography or combination? I haven't found my perfect dance yet, but to tell you the truth, it's in the imperfections of life that inspires me the most. I really don't care if I ever understand the essence of my creativity, because my muse is in the unexpected twists and turns of my journey.

So I'm an out of the box dancer who teaches creative expression that is limitless. If I am to be an example for my students to follow, than I need to lead by experience so I can teach them with the knowledge of a veteran. This is perhaps my certification to my students; limitless inspiration called the ebb and flow of life.

18 - Paying Your Dues

"There is so much more to choreograph with an open mind and open heart that sees the forest for the trees."

For entertainers, as the year's progress, the hardest part of gaining knowledge is recognizing how unrealistic the expectation is, of desiring a money back guarantee for our youth. Unfortunately we age just like everyone else. The fountain of youth changes from an indomitable quest to a journey of enlightenment and understanding. The journey eventually, becomes more important then the end objective. Age shows herself with the jovial contentment of enjoying the view. There is so much more to choreograph with an open mind and open heart that sees the forest for the trees. Because of the length of an older dancer's journey, there is something uniquely beautiful with her choreographies that you don't see with a younger, less experienced dancer. It's as if life showcases itself completely within movements and gestures of older dancers, because they can express themselves with a genuine passion that younger dancers just don't possess. This advantage should create a belly dance world where older dancers are cherished and appreciated but in the real world this is not always the case.

Years ago when the Belly Dance Superstars came onto the dance scene, they changed many things. At first I had no idea who some of the dancers were besides realizing there weren't as many older dancers represented, which would have changed the mix a bit. I was of the impression that dancers who were like my teachers and my teachers- teachers were the superstars. They had years of experience under their belts and that usually meant years of paying their dues that resulted in unquestionable respect.

It seemed as if in the blink of an eye, the Belly Dance Superstars appeared out of nowhere and the rest is history as they say. As a working entrepreneur, I had to take a step back and redefine my view regarding the word superstar. Maybe my assumption of what the word meant was unrealistic. I was looking at the word according to my heroines of belly dance like, Taheya Carioca, Naima Akef, Samia Gamal and Suheir Zaki, just to name a few. The superstars somehow brought the silver screen back to life in eye popping color and the vaudeville days of yesteryear emerged from obscurity thanks to multiple tours, workshops and marketing. Many dancers felt for once, there was a group that could change the opinions and attitudes regarding the legitimacy of our dance form. It wasn't just a start it was a vindication for those of us in the trenches of a prejudicial world.

Years ago, I read about a group of dancers that titled themselves as superstars on their flyers, and because of this, they were ostracized by their dance community for this misnomer. I wrote a blog post about it and at the time I disagreed with the community's bias, but as I look back at that particular post, I now realize that words can be misused. I wouldn't call myself a professor of belly dance anymore than I would call myself a superstar. Titles have to be earned and not used in trivial manners that give the wrong impression of an earned status. Titles are a sign and rank of years filled with trials, tribulations, errors and successes because dancers who have been around the block a few times, have already experienced their rites of passage time and again.

One question that lingers, staring me in the face, is a basic fundamental that seems to have become a twisted macramé, tangled in its infancy. Do women know the icons of their time? Who defines these icons and why weren't the teachers of celebrated dancer's, the ones who paved the way for the superstar generation? Were these dancers too old to be the stars or even in the chorus for that matter? It was in fact, a man who emerged from his podium, creating an enigma with the intention of reselling us our image. To a certain extent I think we bought it hook, line and sinker because as I stated before, we wanted things to change and we hoped that with the new changes our prospects for dancing would be better. The belly dance community as a whole bought the packaged deal, because it looked beautiful and packaging sometimes becomes more important then the product. But let me make myself clear here, there are some of the superstars that take my breath away and they represent the very best belly dance has to offer anywhere. My former question is based on being apart of a multitude of dance communities who have so many stars in their midst's. Look around your community and you will see what I am talking about. We are blessed to have so many women who grace the stages with their talent, skill and authority of our dance form. Let us not forget them because they are the original belly dance superstars.

With women being the majority in our dance field, why we didn't create our own superstar entourage, years ago? Maybe it's because our mortality in this dance is based on certain facts that tend to be hazy at best. The rules get bent or twisted out of shape, because dancers don't want to be passed by and forgotten. You subsequently have dancers who continually strive for a coveted spot in our belly dance folklore. It can be a lonely endeavor because a person's drive sometimes has room for only one. But even if a certain few make it, perhaps their downfall is the fear of being forgotten. If these reining divas had chosen their understudies and helped them become the new leaders of our history, then our outcome would have been a generational melting pot of cultures, styles and education. The superstar tour would have been our lineage and dancers would be vying for their chance to dance in a historical collective of our history in the making. Basically what I am saying here is if women were leading women into the new millennium, this in itself would speak volumes regarding our understanding of each other and our place in history. Are we doing this?

Dancers today, who know their history, hopefully have an understanding that passing it down is the earned right of passage, that years of training bestow on

113

teachers and dancers who have paid their dues. I know what some of you may be thinking; who decides who has paid their dues? I wondered this myself. We don't have a board of directors that we can go to and ask, "Have I made it yet," but on the other hand I don't spend a lot of time worrying about it. I think when we spend less time worrying about getting ahead we will find that in many ways we have already arrived.

A Smack on the Head and a Pat on the Back

Years ago I was asked to teach a workshop in Roswell, New Mexico. At the time, I was hired on pure faith and word of mouth since the studio owners Alice and Mathew didn't know me. When Alice telephoned me regarding the workshop, I went through an emotional roller coaster of, every emotion possible that makes you tingle inside. Following my phone call with Alice, I gave an announcement during class and invited some of my students to come with me to Roswell and perform in the evening show. My Students accepted the invite graciously, except for one student who looked disgruntled when I asked her to join us. Everyone had to pay their own expenses, but it was such a fantastic experience that most didn't want to pass it up. By the end of class, this particular student finally decided to join the group but I could tell she had mixed emotions about it. She had been going to another studio besides mine, and I noticed her loyalty to my studio throughout the weeks had started to wane.

Our first day in Roswell started off with a blast, and we had a great time experiencing a haunted building full of creepy ghosts and dead aliens. That evening we enjoyed a great dinner and my friendship and love for Alice and Mathew was cemented from that day forward. To make a long story short, the Saturday workshop went really well. During the evening dinner show, I experienced an overwhelming sense of pride watching my students perform. But unfortunately, I felt strange vibes coming from my disgruntled student who did a beautiful job of dancing and was a favorite amongst the audience. As I was waiting to be introduced, I let her know how proud I was of her performance and instead giving me the proverbial break a leg well wishes, she said, "My performance will be hard to beat." She smiled at me and walked away.

As my moment to perform came, I forgot about any anxiety, including her comment because I was doing a 30 minute performance. At the end of my show, I received a standing ovation from the crowd, and I felt like I had just won the lottery. It was a surreal evening and one that I cherish to this day. The excitement in the dressing room was contagious, as my students and I congratulated each other on performances well done. As expected my disgruntled student was distant and there were no congratulations from her to anybody. She stayed that way throughout the evening, and the following morning she left early without saying good bye to anyone. She didn't come back to the studio after that, and my phone calls to her were not returned. So fate has a way of patting you on the back and surprising you with a hard smack all at the same time.

Hometown Fame?

I realized that sometimes in our own hometowns, we can become as important as a weed. If you are a weed that flowers, you can at least sustain yourself in an environment that is harsh or dry by looking like a flower of importance. This way, you won't get plucked or pulled from your vantage point. Water like compliments can be at a premium especially when there's no rain and the dry spells can feel like they last forever. This is where you have to do your own rain dance and understand that we don't always pick the best environments to grow in.

This led me to the inevitable file titled, *unanswered questions* that linger in most women's contemplative abyss. First question is, have you ever wondered why it's so hard for someone to get well known in their own hometown? I have, and I have to say, it reminds me of a struggling actress trying to get a bit part in a movie, only to find the parts have been filled. Is it the studio rivalries that creates this, or is it really the need to get a better environment elsewhere, that is richer in opportunities? The latter seems to be more prevalent from my experience, but maybe that's because it's easier to go in blind in a new place, with naïve expectations.. For instance, I can remember the occasional venue that happened in my early years back home. If you were a student striving to perform there were a specific few who repeated the infamous line of, *maybe next time.* I understood this reasoning, especially since there is so much work that goes into producing a show and more dancers than Carter has liver pills to play the parts. But I realized that I would never be a featured performer in a show, if I didn't leave and start fresh some place else. This is why I travelled to other states, because I quickly learned it was easier to audition without struggling to validate my dance to a group of performers who knew me. Of course this feeling could have easily been my own insecurity and need for validation. In the long run, I had the need to move on because of the gypsy in me who craved new places and faces. But in the end, I found that leaving and starting over some place else was a lot easier to handle then waiting for my turn for that golden opportunity to perform that unfortunately never came my way back home. Home became more of a plural definition than singular, because my habit was to pack up and move on every six months. I created my own problems because there was no square one to go back to.

I often wondered why I didn't just create my own venues and dance in them in my early years. I realized that it didn't occur to me because I had the somewhat, accurate impression that only experienced dancers produced shows. As I got older, I realized that we have to start some place and starting from familiar ground would have been simpler and just as good as any other place to start. Looking back, it was obvious I didn't have to pack up and move as often as I did, but then my dance wouldn't have grown in manner in which it did.

Experiencing other dance communities was the best part of growing up in belly dance. I learned that if you want to dance, than you make sure you dance, period!

I teach my students that in our business don't wait till the cows come home for opportunities, stand your ground and grab or create as many chances as you can. The unfortunate result of any hesitation is you might lose out to someone who didn't wait. Creating opportunities for dance in the end was a lot easier than I thought. The only drawback was the weight of responsibility that sat comfortably on my shoulders digging its nails into me.

Hell Hath No Fury Like a Belly Dance Teachers Scorn

Looking back at the opportunities that came my way, made me realize that I paid a price I never intended to pay for my occasional good fortune. The outcome of getting work can play havoc on a dancer's reputation, because women tend to demonstrate a lack of propriety when it comes to their competition.

Years ago when I was just starting out performing publically, I experienced one of my more dramatic dance lessons. I was hired at a Greek restaurant in Beverly Hills, California called the Greek Connection and unbeknownst to me, the owner let two dancers go after hiring me. I didn't know at the time that you should insist on the house dancers being present when you audition, as a sign of respect. As you can imagine, I paid a huge price for my blunder. A few weeks later, early one Friday night, the two dancers cornered me just before I was ready to perform my first show of the night. Instead of talking in the restaurant, they asked me to follow them outside so we could talk privately, so I agreed. As soon as we stepped out the door, they started to berate me and accused me of stealing their gig. As I listened to their heated words, I let them know I was in total agreement with them and understood their anger and resentment towards me. I suggested we all go inside and confront the owner. Within a heartbeat, they froze in their tracks and their complaints went from confrontational to a more appeasing tone. They adamantly made it clear that they didn't want to confront the owner. I felt they had made me the sacrificial lamb for something that wasn't entirely my fault so I told them I was going to confront him anyways.

I marched myself inside the restaurant and headed straight for the owner, tapping him on his shoulder. I told him I needed to talk to him, so he gestured for me to follow him back to his office. Once he sat down behind his desk, I then blurted out everything the girls had told me thinking that I was vindicating myself by doing so. Amazingly, he just sat there looking at me and said, "So what." He continued to say the customers liked me and besides that, I was cheaper than keeping the two of them. At that time he was paying me $35.00 a show, which he said was the going rate. Not only did I believe him, but I unknowingly undercut the dancers who were getting paid much more then me.

I was making my living solely with my belly dancing at the time, so I felt I couldn't just leave his restaurant without having another job to replace his. As I was to find out Karma already had a plan.

A few weeks later, the teacher of the two dancers who I unintentionally undercut, was hired to perform at the restaurant for a celebrity gala event. I was also scheduled to perform that night too. Unfortunately, the owner forgot to tell me he had hired her and didn't need me. As you may have guessed, when I walked in, I was unwelcome and shown the cold shoulder by the girls dance teacher. It was a huge night full of celebrities and fashion designers and I was devastated that I was not dancing. And let me tell you, *hell hath no fury like a belly dance teacher's scorn*. This woman loudly questioned my dance ability in front of everyone, doing a great job of humiliating me on the spot. The wait staff glared at her because I had become good friends with quite a few of them, but the owner on the other hand was angry the moment he saw me. He asked me in a gruff voice what I was doing there. I looked him straight in the eye and said, "I'm here because I never received a phone call from you telling me that I wasn't dancing." He looked at me funny until he finally realized that he had never called me. He said something I have remembered to this day. He said, "It's not my problem you're here. I don't need you tonight, so go home." Just like that, he walked away with no emotion and no shame.

As I left, I unfortunately had to walk past the insulting dancer and as I did, she said something to a group of people and they all started to laugh. It was a hard lesson to learn but it was one that helped me develop back bone and character. I vowed never to step foot in that restaurant again. Two weeks later, I received a phone call from the restaurant owner asking me to come back. I had learned my lesson well and with a more mature tone in my voice, I told him, " I wouldn't come back and dance for you if you were the last restaurant on earth." And with that I hung up.

Each experience can be rich in gut wrenching blows that can make you sick to your stomach. My backbone when I first started out dancing was about as thick as a toothpick. I didn't know elephant skin was a necessity in this business. I learned quickly that paying my dues meant that I was apart of the mainstream agenda whether I liked it or not. Dance is life and to think or expect the two to be separate is a very naïve way of thinking. The rite of passage with paying dues can create a dancer who is a caricature of herself, a dancer for hire with no place to go. We eventually get to that wonderful plateau that takes years of experience and then after achieving this, we find in certain circumstances that we have been passed up for someone more naïve, younger or cheaper.

The Waiting Game

Out of curiosity, I asked a publisher of a dance magazine what it took to be on the cover of her magazine because I had noticed some of the dancers on her covers had come onto the belly dance scene within the last ten to fifteen years.

The editor stated that the dancers who made it on her cover had to make a difference in their community and they had to have a dance style that was respected and well known. It was a good response, and as I had thought. But the problem as I see it, is there are many women who are major players in their community without the celebrity status. Most of them aren't on the covers of magazines because of home choices and personal responsibilities keeping them local to their communities. I realized that the publisher put dancers on her magazine cover that she liked and were in her view the definition of successful dancers. It's as simple as who you know in this business that makes the difference.

Paying your dues can be a very complex ordeal that nobody really has the answers to. Being at the right place at the right time or knowing the right people, can side step this ancient custom of trial and error. On my end, it became apparent that I walked a very isolated path because the right people didn't always walk on the path I was traveling. My fate was sealed in the dos and don'ts of how to become a belly dancer. It was comforting that other dancers blundered along as well, while I occasionally sat on the sidelines. The blunder factor is a lot like Murphy's Law. Add in a slice of arrogance and it can lead a person down a very narrow path where one wrong turn can cause a tumble down a steep incline or off a mountain ledge. As dancers, we always hope for the best but if we were really honest with ourselves, sometimes we hope a particular dancer lands on her face.

Being on the sidelines isn't always the safest place to be but sometimes you have to take a good look at what you are participating in. If you ask me, belly dance drama beats anything on TV. If belly dancers ruled the world it would be the most complicated, interesting and enjoyable planet to be on. I know there have been a few occasions where I placed myself directly at drama's door step, knocking at her furiously to let me in. I could have won an Emmy with my self imposed damsel in distress behavior. Like I said to a waiter who thought I was an actress," *I'm not an actress, I'm a drama queen.*" Aren't we all!

19 - Nickel and Diming a Living

"Becoming the muse for our own creativity when we live as dancers, can take a toll on our dance persona because even she needs a siesta!"

The Questionable Gig

Have any of you ever taken a gig, instinctively knowing that it might not be the best experience, but you did it anyways because you needed the money? I have, and that nagging premonition that was in the back of my mind, always showed itself in various forms of anxiety, dread or panic. After the infamous gig was over, I was always grateful that I survived and I would vow never to take a gig that didn't feel right. I'm not saying, I went and performed in deserted warehouses or scarcely lit bars called "Bubba's". It was the people hiring me that were sometimes questionable, because meeting people in person is an entirely different story than talking to them on the phone. The problem is, that in the back of most belly dancers minds, is a little voice saying, "If you don't take this gig, some other dancer will get it and make the money." But if the gig is questionable the question you should really be asking yourself is, how safe is it?

I danced at bachelor party years ago and deep down, I felt like I didn't know what to expect and I didn't like the unknown feeling. The fiancé of the groom asked me to dance for him, and I felt that since I knew her, it would be safe enough for me to accept the gig. It was the one time, I found out that my sword had many more uses then I had realized. As I was dancing for the groom, the very drunk and boisterous crowd started to chant, "Take it off! Take it off!" He started chanting with them, so I gracefully went towards my sword, picked it up and pointed the sharp end of the sword at his throat and gave him a cold stare that said there would be none of that! The groom stopped the chanting immediately and so did everyone else. Suffice to say, the rest of my show continued without a hitch and I was pleased with myself for standing up for my art form and for belly dancers in general. I was really grateful I was paid in advance, because I'm sure if his fiancé knew what he was up to, he would have been in the dog house for at least a week. I learned from this experience that educating the masses can come in many forms and guises and in this particular instance, it just happened to be the sharp end of my sword.

The Professional Dancer

The unfortunate aspect of this dance is that so many women enthusiastically perform who already have jobs or they dance for next to nothing. Since they don't live off their dancing, they can pick and choose which gigs they want to do. Most decisions are based on individual wants and needs and not a working communities, modus operandi. I have actually found that in today's' day and age, some performers have an unrealistic view of expectations with their dance career. The bona fide dancer is in the minority of professional hobbyists. My hat goes off to the dancers who have made a living with belly dancing and stayed in the business. These dancers have a unique clout that only comes from an endurance of a champion.

Thinking back some years ago, I remember performing at a nightclub around the Dallas area called Sinbads. I heard a knock at my dressing room door and went to see who it was. It was the owner who was informing me that a dancer showed up, who wanted to audition. She wanted to dance my set even though she knew I was getting dressed. He let me know that I had nothing to worry about, and that he was going to tell her to come back later. I told the owner that I wanted to meet her but after my show. I thought it couldn't hurt to see her dance, so I suggested he audition her after my show. When I closed the door, I stood looking at the wall for a minute because I couldn't figure out how a dancer could just walk in and try to take over another dancers gig. My mind raced back to the restaurant in Beverly Hills so many years ago and I wondered if this was another one of *Karma's* pay backs. With this on my mind, I finished getting ready and came out with both barrels ready to fire.

The band heard about the dancer and they seemed to sense my apprehension, so they played beautifully for me, which I greatly appreciated. The dancer was seated at a front table. Her cold stare was obvious, especially since she was glaring at me through out my performance. When my show ended, I quickly went to my dressing room to change and headed out to watch her perform. She was already in costume, so she took her coat off as the owner and I sat down at one of the front tables. Her costume revealed a well proportioned figure and her blonde hair stood out amongst the crowds' predominately black and brown coifed hair. As the band started, it became obvious that she didn't understand the classical music or how to time her approach on the dance floor because she started to dance way too soon instead of waiting for her introduction. The band demonstrated their opinions of her dancing with the first few minutes of her performance. I felt I should give her the benefit of the doubt and started by throwing money over her head. This started the crowd into doing the same thing but by this time, the owner whispered to me that he had seen enough and he got up and walked away. She finished her performance and walked off the dance floor to cool off. I could tell she was trying not to cry, so I picked up the money that was on the floor and walked over to where she was standing, handing it to her. She said I should keep it but I told her it was hers. She smiled at me, and appreciatively took the money then quietly left the club without saying another word. My thoughts immediately went back to the Beverly Hills fiasco and I felt like this was *Karmas* way of giving me a second chance, not only to redeem myself but to give her the compassion that wasn't shown to me.

Verbal Contracts

One of the lessons that I learned early on in my dance career, was that sometimes exemptions to verbal contracts with managers, can catch you off guard and nail you where it hurts the most, your pocket book. On one particular evening, I experienced what I felt was a deliberate indifference from a manager of a nightclub that I used to dance at in Houston. I use to drive from Fort Worth, Texas to Houston, once a month, to work at a wonderful nightclub called *The Mirage*. On one of my scheduled weekends, I was getting dressed for my show in the bathroom. When I came out of the bathroom, the manager told me I was only doing one show that night because he was having another dancer perform the later show. I explained to him that we had an agreement and that it was too expensive to drive from Fort Worth to Houston, to do only one show. He said he was sorry but there was nothing he could do about it. Of course, there was no arguing with him and I realized this was a risky business, where a verbal contract could change without a moments notice.

I did my show and afterwards I saw the dancer, said hello to her in the bathroom and told her I was looking forward to her performance. She was a well known dancer in Texas, so I knew everyone would have a good time watching her perform. As I went to sit down at my table to watch her show, the loud speaker came on with a booming voice introducing her. The lights swirled around and I realized at that moment what if felt to be a peon belly dancer. There were no lights swirling when I went on and they forgot to introduce me that night, which was a first for me since working there.

The music started and she came out with gusto and high energy. The audience applauded, and they seemed excited to see her perform. I was excited too because the energy in the room was electric. But as the moments went by, I noticed a very large group of people start to talk above the music. I was getting a little annoyed with them because they were laughing and talking so loudly that it was distracting. Then something happened that really shocked me, about ten minutes into her show they all got up and started to walk out. There were about thirty or more people in the group so when they got up to leave, they made a lot of noise. One of the women in the group came over to my table and asked why I wasn't doing the last show. I explained they scheduled in another guest dancer to come in, last minute. She bent down to kiss me on the cheek and told me she preferred my dancing. I appreciated compliment especially since she was an Arab woman but I also felt a certain loyalty to the dancer performing. I just felt it was bad manners to leave like that. To my surprise another large group got up and left a short time later, making another loud exit. I had to stand up on a chair because I was way in the back, so I could see the rest of her performance and was irritated by the group's bad timing. I could tell the loud noises affected the performance of the dancer as it would any of us. She finished her show minutes later, and left the stage for the bathroom looking at no one.

That night changed my view of this dancer forever, because later that night, I found out she danced for free since she was a good friend of the managers. In a weird way I feel like we both lost out on that night. I lost out on my second show and the income that would have come with it and she paid a price with an audience's bad timing.

So why would an experienced dancer who should have known better, dance for free? This is a problem that affects our community and professional dancers, who like me are making a living with their dancing. Life has a way of teaching us as we progress down our path and as I became more knowledgeable in my dancing, I learned that my blunders in the past, cost other dancers just as others have cost me. We learn our dance etiquette through trial and error and hopefully in the end we become better dancers and dance neighbors. Being community conscious is a must, for all of us.

Making a Living with our Dancing

Reviewing my past has made me look at what I may have lost along the way on my dance journey. What came to the forefront was very interesting. I found that it had to do with what my community is losing. It is something very sacred and I didn't realize how much I had taken it for granted; it is the right to make a living with our dancing.

Some studios will dance for next to nothing (which I call undermining) just as long as they get the gig. Like I said before, we have to ignore that little voice that says there's not enough work for everyone and remind ourselves this is untrue. If we have to watch our backs with our own community than we have to take a good look at the community we live in.

Years ago, I was hired by a salon to dance for their once a year VIP customer party. I was underbid by another studio who took the gig out from under me. Two weeks before the party it became apparent that the salon was not returning my phone calls. I found out through the grapevine, that they hired the studio dancers for next to nothing and the salon owner never gave me a courtesy call, to let me know. There was no way, I could compete with the studio price or want to. Their low standards inadvertently undermined me besides their own community because setting such a low standard, trickles down and affect all of us. This is one problem that is way too common in dance communities. How can any of us in this business compete with free or low minimal wages?

But you can't always blame others for this problem. Sometimes the carpet is pulled out from under us, and once we hit the ground, we find out that we allowed it to happen. Case in point, students! When the desire to be the center of attention gets a hold of any young dancer, it's usually hard to keep her from leaping out the door. And when that someone is a student, it can be like holding back a genie in a bottle who wants to get out. A good example of this, was when I was dancing at restaurant in Albuquerque a few years ago called Pars Cuisine. One particular weekend, I got a call from some people who wanted me to dance at their party but it was on my regular dance night at the restaurant. I sent out one of my students who had been performing for a couple of years to the party in my stead. One thing that I requested is that she hand out my cards since I was the contact person. Off she went, excited and ready to entertain the crowd. The following day, I called the hostess to see how things went and I was informed by the hostess that my student gave out her cards instead of mine. I didn't tell my student I was going to make a follow up call so I guess she thought I wouldn't know. I don't ask for a percentage but I do expect a certain protocol to be followed. I gave her the benefit of the doubt but eventually realized after another gig, she was becoming my competition and she was doing it right under my nose. So I did what any decent teacher would do, I confronted my student who immediately gave me a song and dance reply when I informed her, she could get her own gigs from then on. The trust was broken and I didn't see it being mended anytime soon, especially when she tried to weasel her way out of it.

The Ego Facade

I was told that a group of dancers in my own home town, years ago, tried to get together and create an alliance or committee, that's sole purpose was to create equal opportunities for working dancers. Unfortunately, opinions and ideologies clashed and the meetings fell apart. But all was not lost, because individual ideas were put into self adaption as well as protocols set by different studios and teachers. At least these women knew what their dance students needed and they implemented their knowledge into their curriculum and education. Students represent more then just themselves on stage, they represent their studios, teachers and community.

It's a given that students need to understand how important training and experience is, but unfortunately there are dancers performing in our midst's, who have no idea the consequences of their actions. Why is there a tendency for some students who take classes for a year or two, to leave solid training to go start their own classes under the guise of "teacher". They mislead their students into thinking they have more experience than they do. I think sharing dance is one thing but advertizing yourself as a full blown teacher is another.

A veteran dancer allows her dance to evolve. It's almost like she sees that time is the spice that makes her dance worth its weight in gold. It all depends on the dancer herself and the value she places on learning her art. The value teachers give to their students is the content of their curriculum. Some students catch on quicker than others but the difference in this dance form is the time frame. You just can't short change experience.

What inexperienced teachers are doing, is taking away and discarding the old ways based on two reasons, either they are indifferent to them, or they don't know any better. Add insult to injury and you have income being taken away from professional teachers and dancers which trickles down to a low income community, struggling to survive in today's economy. The ones who experience this first hand, are the older teachers, not because of their age but because of societies superimposed need for belly dance to be presented in a way so that anybody can teach it.

How can any student know what they are learning if their assumed teacher can't teach them the fundamentals of this dance form? What are they paying for then? Which is worse, not knowing or not caring? An ignorant dancer goes out and represents her community without knowing she is ignorant of the fundamentals and an indifferent dancer doesn't care what she is representing; her agenda is a selfish indulgence. I have lost work because of both types of dancers and I have friends who are dealing with these same issues. Once a dancer learns the ropes, it's important for her to understand how to play nice.

Nowdays, all it takes is marketing and just about anybody can put up a website and create a ruse that they are an expert dancer. So to compete, professional dancers have to learn how to be proficient in marketing themselves. But I have to say, realistically websites just don't cut the mustard anymore. Learning technology and keeping the fires burning are a juggling act that I have learned to embrace by necessity called survival.

The Female Drawback

Whisperings and opinions can take a toll on a community, especially if the modus operandi is to do nothing but complain. This can take precedent over good old fashioned interaction and positive dialogues that create a better world for dancers to live in. I think success would come more easily, if dancers could accept and understand their true feelings concerning their relationships with each other. The formula for a successful strategy has to include, self promotion that focuses solely on the dancer and her unique style of dance. But women can waste time blindly focusing on each others successes or failures, instead of focusing on how to build up their own business. Failure in other dancers is easier to watch because a dancer can gauge her own standards according to her contemporaries' short comings.

Mignon McLaughlin stated it well; *"No woman wants to see herself too clearly."* This is because we might see too much of ourselves in others, especially those we are competing with. In a bizarre way it would be like competing with a nemesis of ourselves of our own creation.

Writing

Writing has been equivalent to being reborn for me because of the freedom to put down thoughts, written or on a computer. In other words, writing has kept my sanity from going off the deep end. Writing articles for dance magazines, has been one of the best ways to get out to our various communities that otherwise wouldn't know me. Thinking back, I can remember whining because I wasn't seeing the content that was important to me in articles regarding the real day to day problems in dance. I don't sew, so I wasn't interested in learning about bras and things of that nature; I was looking for a connection to other dancers who were going through the same problems as me. So my husband suggested that I write articles on what I was looking for, in a way becoming part of a connection and voice for other dancers. What happened after I started to write astounded me, because not only did my name get out into a variety of dance communities, but women began to email me regarding their problems that were similar to my own!

One article in particular, helped me realize that I had created a guilt complex based on feelings that were a natural process of being an entertainer. It wasn't until I had typed my thoughts down in paragraph form, that I was able to see how I was feeling was a response from belly dance being my obsession for so many years. Writing changed my life, and actually helped me get over specific problems and issues that would trip me up from time to time. I realized that more times than not, the problems were in my head and getting rid of them, was a long journey of self evaluation. There is no resolution unless we take stock of who we are as women. The results will vary with time and only then will we gain glimpses of our journey's meaning.

Writing helped me heal and connect with other dancers, besides becoming an intrinsic tool to keep my sanity.

Elissa Melamed stated *"Men look at themselves in mirrors. Women look for themselves."* Our journey is always about finding out who we are. Thoughts and words have power and I found that if I listened to what I was complaining about, I had the ability to fix it, instead of looking to others to fix it for me. The end result was, I became a productive dancer that not only voiced my opinion but I was proactive in finding my own solutions. This was the best advertizing I had ever done and the end result was connecting my name to problem solving not only for myself but for others. Writing also gave me a clout that I didn't have before, and associated my name to the topics of our times. Students have often told me that they were proud of the fact that I wrote for various belly dance magazines. Little did they know it was to keep me sane in an insane business!

Embracing Our Celebrity

This seems to be the one area that trips up a lot of dancers, especially those who come from humble beginnings like myself. Most dancers I have known, at first just want to dance because it is their passion, with no thoughts of a career. Those who make it a career, have to understand that if they don't treat themselves like a celebrity, than nobody else will. Yet in our society, we have this "ego" meter that tends to go off when we see another dancer embrace her own celebrity.

It's a hot topic to say the least because let's face it, there is usually one dancer that bugs the heck out of us, at any given time who thinks she is the cats meow. But my friends and I don't go around with our "ego" meter stuck out in front of us, measuring everyone else's self importance. If one of us gets a big head, we actually make fun of each other and the laughter keeps us humble and grounded. If we don't laugh at ourselves, we can become the antithesis of our own good will by throwing verbal daggers with a marksman's aim. Within communities, dancers tend to compete with those closest to them in their own neighborhoods. So, it's important that we work together to ensure our lives, as well as our communities aren't drama based and ripe for a reality show. There is always a script waiting to happen, so it's up to us to become the writers, directors and producers of our own story so it doesn't end up in someone else's script with exaggerated tales.

Another faux pas that can happen with our celebrity is, when dancers could care less who you are until they know who you are. An example of this was when I was asked to dance for a show that was going to benefit a kid's troupe in my hometown. I was in a back room getting dressed along with a bunch of other dancers, who had come in from out of town to dance in the show. I tried conversing with them but they shuffled off responses that were short and curt. So I eventually stopped trying and finished putting myself together.

Just as I was about finished getting dressed, the producer of the show walked in the dressing room and asked if we had introduced ourselves. They didn't really say yes, so she introduced me and told them who I was. Once the producer stated my name, all of a sudden, they all started to talk to me as if I was someone of importance. I was a bit flustered and I would have to say bugged that my name changed how they reacted to me. I know what some of you may be thinking, it was nice my name was recognized. Yes to a certain degree it was but on the other hand, since we are all occasionally in the same boat together which tends to happen a lot, wouldn't it be better to get to know each other just for the sake of getting to know each other? Worth is just a metaphor if dancers can't see the value in each other.

I must admit that at various times in my dance career, I have felt awkward relating and conversing with dancers in this business. A glass of wine or two always seemed to make those laborious moments of figuring out how to relate to people, more palatable. I didn't know where I stood most of the time in my community, and I was uncomfortable with this isolating factor. Eventually I just allowed myself to be comfortable in my own skin. This allowed me the luxury of filling in the blanks regarding my own title and self worth. I had to put away my ego meter even for myself because otherwise, I wouldn't have accepted my own worth. As a dancer, I naturally tend to create a world inside me, while I live in the outside world. If I live in a constant state of what I create, than hopefully, the two worlds merge together and become one or the big bang happens, and chaos ensues. Humility can allow us to merge into anything just as long as we know the truth of who we are. Celebrity is only a state of mind.

The End Result of Marketing

As I was performing at various restaurants and night clubs, I noticed that the customers always wanted a trinket or personal memento from me, to take home with them. I started to give out autographed 4x7 photos of myself to fans and at the same time, I gave out my business cards which seemed to mean more because they were connected to a photo. My calendar started to fill up within a few months and continued to stay that way. When I asked people how they got my number, they would tell me I autographed one of my photos for them along with my card. Giving people a way to remember you is very important, especially with so many dancers looking for work. People always remember a celebrity and in our business this is how we stay alive. At times, I have fought being a success in this dance form because I'm caught between the artist in me and the career woman. One thing I do know is that if I don't become a success according to my own standards and aspirations, than I only have myself to blame. In life, it's not only about   playing with a full deck of cards but knowing how to play the game. Just remember that having a few aces up your sleeve comes in handy, especially when the table of life has players who know the game just as well as you. A few of those players are called lessons, drama, time and karma. Ultimately remember that the main person we play against is ourselves. The aces up our sleeves are our convictions, principles and values we bring with us into our dance and in the end, we realize that the game of success is really won within ourselves.

20 - Teaching a Philosophy Way of Dance

"Combining all of life experiences, lessons learned and not learned creates the most beautiful design of all; the individual dancer."

The unanswered questions of my youth, have stayed with me all these years and at times, not only became a worthy adversary but became an unintentional teacher. Later on, the lessons I wanted to share with my students occasionally came back to bite me in my "you know where." This was because various students were so preoccupied in getting the move or combination, that they turned deaf to my assumed wealth of information. But maybe my wealth of information was only in my mind and not theirs. My foundation was built on *my* lessons in life and at times, my students didn't know where I was coming from. Even more so, my students couldn't appreciate how I learned my lessons because they were so self absorbed in their own learning process, which is natural.

Watching this process, made it obvious to me that I had to help my students find their own glue or stability for their own foundation. But as I found out this was easier said then done. Looking back at the beginning years of my dance career, I saw that I didn't separate my lessons of achievements from my feelings of failure. Anything that I held dear to my heart or deemed unnecessary, was thrown together inside my imaginary traveling pouch without a thought or care to the consequences. This isn't human nature but human habit, so I eventually did an internal house cleaning and threw out everything that didn't serve me anymore.

Being a teacher is more than just creating a curriculum for students, it's a position that requires thinking in terms of individual self growth for each student. I saw it was necessary to understand how women felt about their dancing, including their self identity in order to help them create a strong structure that would survive the tests of time. The four cornerstones are the most important aspect for any dancer, because they hold her up and keep her structure from failing her. But the draw back is that as the four cornerstones are holding up individual foundations, the individual dancer is also constructing and adding to them at the same time. As a result, it was obvious when some students would come to class with one of their corner stones off balance because they couldn't focus on even the simplest of moves.

Attitudes would enter in the picture, and there's nothing worse than a woman with an attitude waiting to happen. As a teacher, I had to be quick on the draw with appeasing agitated tempers with calming words. So in class, I would remind my students that they had to center themselves **before** they came to class. When they would forget to focus on their four cornerstones, the world around them would affect their creativity, pulling them in a direction they never intended to go. Part of a teacher's job, is to teach students to dance out any issues and feel the resolution in their movements.

So how do we remind ourselves to stay centered? It's a question I have thought about, through out my dance career. The only way I found that I could help my students, was to understand how I put my four cornerstones together and then look at why I unintentionally pick them apart. Since most women perform at all levels of creativity, I found it was important to label each cornerstone so that it was easier to see each one individually. I came up with the names, emotional, physical, spiritual and mental. Looking at each one individually, I think in the long run helps to see clearer what the problems are.

Emotional

As women, our emotional state can fluctuate like a yo-yo on a daily basis. It's a given that when students walk into a studio, they bring their issues and problems with them. Sometimes a person's emotional intensity can work in their favor, but it's a toss up if they fall apart in the middle of practice. I have seen women come to venues, carrying the weight of their emotional problems on their shoulders. The weight of the problem shows up immediately in the flow of their dance. If your emotions are tangled up, then the flow of your dance can become stagnant. On the other hand, if a dancer can take an issue and use the emotional impact to her favor, she will be able to wrap an audience around her fingers. A dancer that does this, can use the force of her emotions to bring her audience to a heightened state of amazement.

I experienced a little bit of this when I was the Dragon slayer in the last theater show I co-produced. I jumped in to play the part at the last minute, which meant I had to become skilled with a light weight aluminum shower rod (aka a magical cane) within six weeks, besides learning the choreography. I had no idea until I started practicing with the shower rod, how dangerous it could be. My misguided aim left huge bruises on my legs and my twirling left much to be desired. The evening of the show, I was a nervous wreck and to top it off, I didn't get a chance to practice the day before the show. As I was performing, I could sense the children in the audience, because their energy was electric and they seemed transfixed by the fight scene between the dragon and me. When I killed the dragon, you could hear loud gasps, and then a huge applause. My raw nerves gave me the boost I needed in the end, because my emotional state helped me get into character. But I have to say, it stands out as the one performance of my dance career that flashed before my eyes. I don't remember much about it except that I lived through it.

Physical

There are many reasons why dancers are attracted to belly dancing. For some, it is a calling that is far reaching into the soul. For others, it is a way to stay in shape, have some fun and make new friends. Most women enjoy the freedom that belly dance offers them from everyday life. But I have found there is another reason, one that women keep hidden away out of fear, called inadequacy. This well kept secret in time, comes out of the closet in class, liberating the student's body image and as a teacher it's the best part of teaching. Even though we know feeling inadequate is validating a non-realistic lie, there's a part of us that believes in this lie perpetuated by what magazines and the media tells us. There has not been one beautiful woman who has come to study with me, that didn't have one issue or another. How distorted our lives become, depends on how distorted we see ourselves in the mirror and how much of this distortion we believe in. When a dancer is in a beautiful state of grace, she is sheer perfection. But if a dancer compares herself to everyone around her, she'll not only demean her own efforts but she'll never rise above her own adversity.

I had a student who was young and a fast learner. She was so hungry for every possible experience she could get her hands. I created as many opportunities as possible for my students and she took advantage of as much as she could. As performances and haflas came and went, I saw her change from a gracious dancer to an unappreciative diva. Unfortunately within a short period of time, she forgot about everybody else except herself. Her heart was full of the momentary applause of her efforts, but her fear of failure was making a toxic brew that was hard for me to deal with as a teacher. Beauty without humility can turn ugly in a heart beat. Physical beauty will only take a person so far. Dance will either illuminate beauty to it's brightest or magnify the cracks of insecurity to it's depravity. Sometimes the physical cornerstone stays weaker than the rest because we never befriend ourselves. If we make other people pay a price for what we aren't willing to see in ourselves, then we counter any progress we make in life.

Spiritual

This spiritual cornerstone seems to clarify everything that we do in our dance. If we neglect this particular corner stone, the consequences become like a depleted feeling with no peace of mind. Our purpose is taken away and our dance becomes empty. The depth of each dancer's convictions, comes from her belief system. I know I can't do a good job of dancing, if my soul is heavy with burdens. This is the one corner stone that many dancers depend on, when all else fails. Spirituality is the part of our dance that holds up even when the other corner stones falter. It is also the main part of our dance that makes us come alive, especially when we find ourselves in the real world of competitive circumstances, dramas and conflict. I don't think we ever really leave it all behind when we dance but somehow dance makes life lighter and less intimidating, at least for those brief moments on stage. The true magic of this cornerstone happens when we get off stage because issues seem less intense and traumatic. It's really about learning how to breathe life into our dance, by celebrating and dancing it on stage. At the end of a performance, the aftermath of problems seems to ease, leaving a feeling of renewed hope in the dressing room.

With our connection to loved ones, it's obvious there is never a time when we are alone on stage. This is the benefit of the spiritual corner stone; it's our empathetic connection to loved ones.

Mental

There have been a few times when I felt that my mind was trying to take over my dance. Sometimes, I feel my mind confusing my body making the most basic choreography seem difficult. The mind can be very important in dance but sometimes it can make us too technical. Dancer's who capture their audiences the most, are the ones who flow with their choreography. Our mental cornerstone is needed to keep us "sane" through out the learning process. But this one can also zone us out. Your right becomes your left and body parts get all mixed up. Interestingly enough, our mind remembers those great moves that combined together, created a dynamic and memorable performance. Ultimately for dancers, they know that the body is the main focal point for the audience and in the end it usually knows what to do.....most of the time. Within the performing process sometimes putting your body on automatic helps the brain take a siesta. But I have to say, on more than one occasion after a performance, my brain sarcastically asked me how I did.

The Glue

A person's individual philosophy eventually comes in and becomes the glue that holds everything together. Combining all of life experiences, lessons learned and not learned creates the most beautiful design of all; the individual dancer. This means that life's journey and experiences make dancers what they are. And yet because of our calling, as dancer we are never fully defined. We represent who we are as human beings on stage that constantly change from one choreography to the next.

"I am not an accumulation of what happens because of human nature, I am an accumulation of my life's lessons thus learning what I want to become."

Leyla Najma

Accepting yourself the way you are, is a major component in the glue that holds together your four Cornerstones. We all want to be well thought of by others but first we must think well of ourselves. Being conscious and aware, strengthens the glue of all the corner stones. The gift back is a constant flow of creativity that allows us to dance our individual lives' up on stage. The exchange is worth all our vulnerabilities, fears and phobias because the end result is being in a state of grace that feels like a little bit of heaven!

21 - The Solo Performer

"Life speaks to dancers, specifically in music and how we dance to her says so much about how we hear her."

I have found the greatest joy in performing solo and feel lucky that I teach solo performers. It is not easy being in the frontline of a dancer's ambitions, because there have been times I have felt I was trampled without warning. The definition for ambition says it's a strong desire or feeling of wanting to be successful in life and to achieve great things. With this being said, I am going to suggest that belly dance teachers be ahead of crocodile handlers and lion trainers in the "Worlds most dangerous jobs!"

When I started to teach years ago, I really enjoyed teaching classes and helping women get their groove on in belly dance, but even more so I enjoyed watching women discover their own talent for dance. Self discovery is a wonderful way for women to heal and gain self confidence, besides spiritually re-awakening their souls. Once this happens, the flood gates of creativity and inspiration come roaring in like a tidal wave and there is no turning the flood gates back. So imagine for a moment, teaching women who are full of this creative energy week after week, it's pretty amazing to watch them fill up their reservoirs with dance.

Once women step up and say they want to dance, change ensues and hidden desires start to emerge. It's not so much that women who dance create choreography only with technique; they are pulling in and forming their passion into every movement. Each dancer is like an atom bomb, waiting to explode on stage. This is why teaching solo performers is so exciting and at the same time a little like walking on egg shells. Anticipating creative outbursts can be a mute point because they can happen at any given time.

"The mediocre teacher tells. The good teacher explains. The superior teacher demonstrates. The great teacher inspires."

William Arthur Ward

As I became more invested as a teacher, I had to make sure that I didn't lose myself while giving as much as I could. Sometimes students will take and forget to give back; perhaps I did this too as a young student. An epiphany changed my perception of students when I realized that eventually the dancer has to be called upon by the student and until that moment happens, we have to patiently wait for this self discovery. Working with solo performers is a lot like molding clay. Eventually a glimmer of an image can be seen of what the student will become. Then the emergence of the dancer within time leaps out and completes the sculpture and gives it detail. This is what a solo performer is; she is the end result of her own design and inspiration.

To be a solo performer means we have to believe in our talent and the depth of our ability. If we dance in doubt, not only will it show in our movements but our energy or creative motivation will be off balance before we ever walk on stage. There is no one to hide behind or beside if a solo performer is having an off night. The solo performer's vulnerability is out in the open, and sometimes the imagination can create a sentiment equivalent to egging on a wild animal with only a feather as protection. Stakes can be high when we create our own dance, because like any artist, there are always those few in the shadows who take it upon themselves to demonstrate negative bias. Back in the dressing room, we can all sense the approval or disapproval of our hard work by the intensity of a silence that is deafening or a verbal congratulatory remark that offers us only a momentary reprieve. Yes, it is brief because there is always choreography to create and another performance waiting to happen.

I have wondered throughout the years, why certain dancers are destined to become solo performers and others to dance in troupes. It never was a calling for me to perform within a troupe though I love the camaraderie. I have always wanted to mold my movements according to how the music moves inside me and through me. Perhaps that is why I prefer to teach solo performers, because I understand the need to constantly create an individual validation of how a dancer sees the world.

It's my way of speaking out about the world around me in a way that is not misinterpreted by words. Words as I have come to experience, can take on a connotation that was never implied by me but misunderstood by any one person, based on their own state of emotions. Dance is raw, so it has nothing to gain except a visual acceptance of what it is. Regardless if people like our performance or not, they visually focus on us for a few brief moments while we are performing. Whether they understand our message, is really secondary to the freedom of being on stage and voicing our opinions of life through our dance.

The Self Serving Personality

Solo performers can come into the studio with hidden phobias that aren't always easy to see. There definitely seems to be a dual personality trait that comes alive after a while. The first trait of most students walking in a studio is that of a gracious learner, which usually lasts as long as their sincerity. The greatest blessing given to a teacher is a student who shares herself discoveries by dancing them, integrating them into her dance persona and succeeding at what she loves. The contradictory aspect to this blessing is the self-serving personality.

The self-serving personality doesn't usually come out until a dancer feels she has wagered in enough experiences under her belt. It's not so much that the drama queen arises from her slumber; it's more like a starlet wanting the main role because she feels she deserves it. The one problem with self- serving dancers is they can't see beyond their own efforts. Once they get to a plateau of comfort, they immerse themselves into their own creativity to a point that blinds them.

Ultimately, they can't see beyond their own rights of passage. It's a handicap that some solo performers experience; basically they have to learn how to contribute to their communities. This is a problem that can't be self medicated because the end result affects communities as a whole. Performances that are remembered in a good light by other dancers will usually be remembered, garnering the chance to perform in more shows down the line. This isn't always the case if the sense of being owed something is lingering in the air, especially in a dance field that is already full of cautious protocol.

I have witnessed the self-serving personality in a few of the shows I jointly produced. The difference between troupe mentality and the solo attitude is obviously on opposite sides of the dance spectrum. The troupe dancers who participated in the shows, went way beyond the call of duty because they wanted the outcome of their efforts to be successful for each other. This has to do with their sense of responsibility to each other; one person's actions would affect the outcome of the whole troupe. Sometimes a solo dancer can't see beyond her own contribution because it is a guaranteed offering she can take to the bank. If responsibility lies continually, only with the self, than the concern for the progressive and creative concept for the whole matrix doesn't exist. I'm not saying all solo performers are selfish, just that a few have this trait down to a tee.

Equality in some ways can go out the window if a solo performer feels her time and effort is being compromised. Self creativity can be a double edged sword, especially when solo performers forget that everyone is creating just like they are and no ones artistic efforts are more important then anyone else's. I found one common element to the solo performer; they evaluate their performance first and then they question the end result of a shows success or failure second. They want to know how their performance rated or compared with everybody else's. It can be no other way, because the solo performer is dealing in a state of creative isolation. Even music that is shared with other dancers, is eventually taken to be molded and shaped into a dancer's interpretation of its meaning. Troupe performing and even duets have the distinction of being created and designed so that their movements are unified, and integrated into the outcome of the whole. Each dancer carries a piece of the design so as they perform together, they complete the artistry of the choreography.

In my contemplative quest, I have come to realize that I have experienced the solo performer's solitary and creative absorption of self. Fortunately, with life's lessons, painful and joyful, I gradually morphed into an altruistic dancer. Since I am speaking in regards to my past faux pas, critiquing the state of mind of a solo dancer is easier because I know her well. It comes down to swallowing the pill of self evaluation and truth and seeing me for who I am.

As time progressed, I have realized that solo performing affected my self definition of what dance is for me. It directed me, even though I thought I was following the ebb and flow of life, called the divine inspiration. The numerous nudgings from creativity have pushed me towards experiences that I never intended to go through, yet in order to complete my dance persona, they were necessary. That's why I find it interesting when dancers want to take a short cut in this dance field, because if lessons aren't learned early on, they will wait around corners when a person least expects them.

The lessons I have learned made me realize that at the end of the day, if I can't find my humility, then I've lost the meaning of what this dance signifies all together.

Russian Roulette

This being said, there is another side to the solo dancer that makes her a critical, over bearing mother that damns her own choreography before it is born out of her. The interesting thing here is, the fact that belly dancing for most women doesn't guarantee success will happen; it's the slight chance it might, that keeps them going. It's like Russian roulette for the nerves, because there is always the chance that our performance bombs or triumphs. The moment just before each performance, can feel like the trigger is being pulled. The results after any performance can be a self created set up. In the end we have to look at our own driving force and why we are really dancing.

Evolving in dance can lead a solo performer on a quest to look for answers, ideas and inspiration, in some cases taking precedent over the original motivations to dance. The revolving door scenario stems from students coming and going from a multitude of studios.

Solo performing is a statement that tells the audience where a dancer is in life, not just what level of dancer she is. If a performer is inharmonious in her own environment, then her ideologies will become unbalanced. A discontent dancer will eventually continue on in dance, with the revolving door syndrome becoming a way of life, validating what is blindly overlooked. If issues are constantly being swept under the rug, than women are learning dance from a disadvantage. Performer's views of their own dance can eventually look sullied based on skewed perceptions. Sweeping issues under a rug and then trying to hide them is futile anyways, because eventually in the end, all issues come out into the open. Belly dance is an art form of expression that states how we really feel about our lives. All issues tend to show themselves in various gestures of the arm, the undulation with a turn or a drum solo that says either you are in control or out of control.

Belly Dance Manual

We don't have a specific school for this dance form but some teachers do call their studios, schools but there is no official book or curriculum that is recognized by all dancers that is the one and only official belly dance manual. A new problem has arisen, because there are so many different styles and fusions now, so how do we put the new with the old? The solo performer is placed in a position that requires her to be proficient in more than one style. Some styles are a variety of fusions integrated with a teacher's preference for expressing her dance. There is a tendency with solo performers to teach their version of belly dance, mixed in with their taste in cultures and music. The changes are such fast transformations, that they remind me of a horse race with fusion and interpretive belly dance, neck to neck, in the lead.

It's a fact, that there are many dancers from all over the world, whose reputations and credentials represent the finest and most educated dancers teaching and representing belly dance today. Without them, our dance would not be what it is today. I know it's unrealistic but if all the amazing dancers of our time could get together, the belly dance manual could be born. It would be like Greek mythology coming to life with all the immortal movers and shakers, creating visionary and relevant passages of our time. Is it unrealistic to want this for the future of belly dance? It depends on where dancers feel belly dance is heading and if its future is in jeopardy.

The Curriculum Thief

I have dance friends whose students unbeknownst to them, started classes with their curriculum being taught verbatim without their knowledge. It's like one day you notice a student is missing and then a few weeks later, you hear about new classes starting up down the street. The dilemma created by some students going off and teaching dance classes, is their inexperience they pass on to their students. They want to be a dance teacher but not by proxy. This is definitely the oxymoron of our times because how else do we learn? If communities don't have standards for such matters, then just about anyone can gain a false status, almost buying their way into a dance field that takes years to learn and perform, there are no short cuts, plain and simple.

Rivalry and Equality

As a solo performer I have often wondered through out the years, why I have stuck to this dance form as a soloist? There's really no easy answer because it's complicated and simple at the same time. The answer has become more visible with age because it's a dance form that has merged into with my life. I embraced belly dance by placing it way beyond an infatuation, making it a way of life.

As I have lived this dance, I have seen in some instances the lack of respect for those who have carried the dance torch for years. There has to be something said for dancers who have been in the business for years who are not as well known as those who are continually in the lime light. Competitive rivalry has been apart of our dance form through out history and still leaves its mark today. I have always felt that if we had a traditional mix of etiquette that changes with the needs of women, belly dance would be up on the times. So then, our competitive spirit that has plagued us for so long, needs to be traded in for an understanding that this dance can be a statement of who we are as women; not individually but as a whole.

With the constant eternal circle pointing us along our path, has there been a change maybe we didn't see. Have we lost our traditions or has the meaning of community faded away with the years? I often think of flowers on a hilltop because when we see a profusion of color, do we stop and look at one flower or do we see the full array of color, showcased in front of us? Flowers can teach us so much because of their wordless declaration to each other that says, we are all equal in significance and beauty. They co-exist with each other for the benefit of the whole group. As a solo performer, sometimes we have to bloom and become one with our community besides being that individual flower. Maybe our communities in dance are really more a value system where we find similar ideals and values with each other. It makes sense because isn't this what studios are really based on? If we can get past the self absorption that takes place with solo creativity, than I think our contribution to the dance world will appear more like a kaleidoscope of sharing.

22 - From Student to Wise Woman

'The wise woman dances from a place of complete acceptance."

The Addiction

Imaginary short cuts can be enticing, especially if a student gets it in their head they can get the fundamentals down faster by beating a self imposed time limit. There seems to be ideas of fame and fortune that are based on romantic notions and unrealistic expectations. An idea or thought about something, is different than experiencing it first hand. The one thing in life I have learned, is that nothing ends up the way I think it will, unless I have the inclination to intend the outcome first. The funny thing is, even though something as simple as intention can be right in front of me, most of the time I never think about it.

The excitement of learning a new dance form, added with those amazing feelings of accomplishment, can alter anyone's ideas of what dance is like as soon as they walk in the studio doors. Add in friendships, workshops and shows and this dance form can consume the life of any unsuspecting aficionado of dance. It's only natural for students to want to speed things up so they can participate and be apart of performing, but it's also important as a teacher to help students understand that dance must be learned in its own time. As teachers if we don't watch the aspirations of each student, negative experiences can come to into the picture before a student has the experience to deal with it professionally. With dance, there are a variety of venues with certain protocols that students need to learn, "first" before they can go out and represent not only the studio but an ethnic melting pot of cultures and traditions.

As teachers we share our own personal experiences from our journeys in dance and we shape and mold our curriculum accordingly. Experience is a key element that is the fine line between teacher and student. Try explaining a ride on a rollercoaster without ever having experienced a rollercoaster. Unless you have a wild imagination, it's hard to do. It's better to experience the rollercoaster and speak from the exhilaration of the actual ride itself. Dance can be similar to the first experience of riding a rollercoaster because the intense exhilaration of performing for people can be an adrenalin rush. How do we explain to a student what the emotional rollercoaster of a negative experience is like? Sometimes emotions are meant to be felt without an explanation but in dance this doesn't work, because we need something to help us gauge possible scenarios.

Becoming a teacher really means that as performers, we have to find ways to explain these feelings so students can get a glimpse of an experience. An important aspect of explaining situations to students is helping them face adversity, so they can continue on with their destiny in dance. This is what puts into place that fine line between teacher and student, those who walk their path understand that in all experiences there is always something to learn. In this regard, it's easier to teach knowing our own limitations and strengths. The experienced dancer will see her own faults; work on changing them instead of blaming others. An experienced dancer faces her fears and adversities by constantly competing with herself. Once a dancer learns to focus on her strengths and weaknesses, she can then understand where she is in her dance. As teachers, this helps us prepare our students to work towards goals created to better themselves by competing with their own strengths and weaknesses. From the beginning of their journey, students have to know the truth about how they really look as a dancer. An untrue compliment given at a time when a student needs guidance the most can create a false sense of achievement that can trip up a student down the road in the harsh reality of entertainment.

On the other side of this coin, is the sought after compliments that are a testament and validation of a performance well done. I have watched students who had great potential look to the applause as an indicator of their worth giving them a false sense of accomplishment. Advice and guidance goes out the window because of the intoxicating allure of becoming recognized. The first symptom is barely noticeable but it quickly becomes evident, especially when you see your words going in one ear and out the other before you've even completed a sentence. The culprit is a tasty treat that quickly becomes addictive for most dancers called celebrity. But once this becomes the focal point, attitudes and dreams morph from the authentic inspired desire to an unrecognizable version of the dancer herself.

Choreography Credentials

Pulling together movements that complete a specific choreography, making it either authentic or contrived is apart of becoming a performer. How well choreography is taught, says so much about the teacher but even more so it says a lot about a student's dedication to her own dance. Here lies a problem, at any given time a student can state that a learned choreography is hers because it is her creativity giving it life. In truth, choreography is given life by each individual dancer who performs it on stage; it's the original design of the inspiration that can't be taken. This is not always easy to understand as a student but communication can become diluted with misunderstandings regarding anybodies creative work. Once choreography is taught to students, I feel it becomes their interpretation of how they understand the movement we teach them, but this doesn't make it theirs. In this instance, the beauty with troupes is that each dancer is to some degree her own presenter of the same choreography.

This is the difference between teacher and student; the teacher is the originator of the inspiration that becomes choreography. She allows her students to mold the movements of her choreography to their bodies so they can understand her inspiration and dance it authentically their way. The metamorphosis from student to choreographer happens when a student takes movement and choreographs her own masterpiece, because only then will she understand that no matter who performs her choreography, it will always be her original, inspired thought.

The Missing Link

Sometimes students can hide their weaknesses to a point to where you can't detect problems, even with the most sophisticated radar. Years ago, I had a student come into my studio that had the unequivocal passion and desire to become a professional belly dancer. As time passed, I watched her in class, and saw there was something missing with her execution of the combinations but I couldn't quite put my finger on it. When I would watch her perform, I saw she had no reaction to her dance. Her face was blank and she had no clue that her expression helped set the mood for her audience. After a few months she left my studio to continue her study elsewhere and I wasn't able to figure out how to help her before she left. A few years later, I watched her perform at a local Hafla and saw the still hadn't learned how to show emotion in her face. She had the same disconnected look which made her blank expression look emotionless. This can make any audience uncomfortable because they need to see the correlation between performing choreography and feeling the dance. Without this connection the audience will eventually get bored. I thought of taking her aside and talking to her, but I knew that she didn't ask for my opinion. Knowing artists like I do, they can get defensive and deaf when advice is given without permission so I decided not to.

Unfortunately students view vulnerability as a sign of weakness which is far from the truth. The best performances I have seen have come from dancers who were scared or nervous because they danced with an explosion of adrenalin on stage. They became a definitive symbol of vulnerability that frees them from anything contrived. Just before a dancer steps foot on stage, divine inspiration takes over prompting the immortal dancer to come out and take over. Their vulnerability seems to open the door to creative authenticity.

The Distorted View

Students can come in and without a moments notice; scramble our views of dance because their paths are based on different sets of principles and values. On occasion, I have had my dance path turned upside down, with me looking at life from the ground up. Personal problems can obstruct a student's ability to see her own beauty, taking away her sanity.

A former student came to a performance of mine with a group of her friends. I noticed immediately that she was not her normal self, at least from what I experienced in and out of class. She was talking in the middle of my show, so I put my hand to my lips and let her know in a joking manner, it was impolite to talk while someone was performing. After my show, I went over to talk to her and it was immediately apparent that there was something wrong. The next day

140

as I was driving home from doing errands, she called me and proceeded to yell at me, exclaiming that I embarrassed her in front of her friends. What I found out later was she had a drinking problem and she was on a strict diet plan with a personal trainer. She didn't tell her trainer about her drinking and the yoyo diet she was on made for a bad concoction of hormones and a low calorie diet mixed with alcohol. The funny thing was I was having a great day and found her phone call the pot hole in the road of my perfect drive. This was one instance where a student tried to impart her distorted view of her world into my lap. I let her know that my view of the world was fine and I gave her back her view without me in it.

The Gamble in Teaching

A wonderful mentor of mine, Romana Frasson taught me a lesson in teaching that I will never forget. She said, I had to teach from experience and the heart in order for my students to believe in me. Sometimes this can be a double edged sword because when we put so much of our passion into our classes, we can lose ourselves in the lesson. Once a student learns her teachers curriculum, understanding the lessons and methodology, she than becomes the end result of a joint effort.

I have dance friends who have taught students for years, and all of a sudden, I'll notice the students are gone. Out of sight, out of mind becomes precedence over what once was a huge part of their dance training and life. It's almost as if the years of mentoring become lost on the side road of obscurity. Looking back at some of the students who left my studio, I haven't heard a peep from them and I occasionally see them. Sometimes we just have to let it be and know everybody is where they need to be.

When a student becomes disloyal to a teacher, it's usually a residual statement of how their lives are going. It's apart of the mix that creates spontaneous choices, that weight down their emotional baggage. Having compassion is a necessary element in being a good teacher, especially when we witness our students processing, learning life and dance as they travel on their paths. I must say, sometimes they see us do the very same thing. This is one of those topics where there are two sides to every story. Personally, every student that I have taught, I didn't expect them to thank me when they left, on good terms or otherwise. I taught them because it is what I do and in the end, I always learned something.

When we dance for no other reason but to just dance, the passion for dancing becomes more then just a goal. As I have matured in life, I have come to realize that my passion for this dance was really a false front that hid my desire for deeper insights into my soul's journey. Dance touched who I was and every time I was in my souls company, I felt complete and whole.

Dancing was an obvious tool that helped me understand my soul's journey eventually allowing me to ease up on questioning my path. Since it's taken me so long to get to my place of understanding, I've realized that as a teacher, I can't afford to judge anyone walking through my front door. This is because no one can know the true story of each and every student who studies with them…it's a gamble and one that we have to make whole heartedly. If we don't, we go against the grain of what this dance is all about. Ultimately, it came down to this; sometimes I came out a winner and other times I lost. Sometimes verbal descriptions are a way student's place imaginary approval or disapproval marks on our studio doors. That part is definitely the gamble.

The Spirit of Dance

The energy that dancers create in a dressing room, is the exchange that brings out the spirit of the dance in a show. This exchange of energy is very unique and it directs the audience's senses and emotions to a heightened state of awareness, to a point they might not even be aware of. I don't think people know they are actually experiencing the ancient soul of belly dance, in her truest form. In a way, I had to come full circle to understand this, also realizing that dancers are not only the gateway for the soul of belly dance, but they are also her gate keepers. The dressing room can become consecrated ground for many or it can become a place of hostility for others. I have seen and felt both, wondering how the two extremes can live side by side with each other. They are almost like sisters, one is day and one is night. This is the aspect of belly dance that makes her so exciting, because she can be like a box of chocolates; the unknown can be as intoxicating as savoring the flavor within each bite.

In looking back at some of my students, I found this business is based on a balancing act of ego and determination. This dance attracts all age groups so it is only natural for women, who are older in age, to want to embrace their own ability, regain certain aspects of their youth and some sort of celebrity on stage. There doesn't seem to be immunity from self indulgence in creativity. In all entertainment there tends to be a mix of women who want more, craving the limelight for as long as they can dance. In this type of melting pot of want and want more, the recipe can become never enough.

Those who prefer to dance along side others, become satisfied with the joys of performing, allowing the experience of dance to fill them creatively.

Youth can be an advantage in this dance form, because there tends to be a stronger tenacity to come back time and again from adversity. Yes those who have been dancing many years, have experience to back them up which can be just as powerful. For older dancers, emotional experiences showcase themselves in greater detail with the wear and tear of life, shows more as we get older. Continually getting up and shaking ourselves off after we have experienced a particular hardship can become an old habit, but as we get older the bruises seem to last longer. Interestingly enough, the teacher can wear her emotions to her advantage and if a student is lucky enough, she can observe her teacher perform from an authentic and knowledgeable place that only comes with time. It's almost like time bestows the experienced dancer with a privileged grace. This type of grace creates an enticing synergy that showcases dance in a timeless consciousness. This leads to dancing life on stage, with no apology or the need to defend one's own creativity, which is the ultimate goal most dancers seek on their path. It is this freedom, which allows older dancers to be themselves on stage without asking for validation. In the end, the wise woman dances from a place of complete acceptance. Anyone who wants to rival a dancer's freedom on stage truly doesn't understand where their dance comes from or their identity as a dancer.

The balance of life includes the balance of our body's energy and knowing where our center of power comes from. It was a place foreign to me in my younger years. I remember the day, I found my sacred space because it was the first time I stood my ground on my dance beliefs.

If we aren't careful, our temple can become desolate and abandoned, reflecting back to us the empty thoughts of forgotten feelings, that affect our ability to dance from a centered and balanced place of refuge. I thought that dance was the catapult for finding my sacred space, but she is the end result of my accumulated knowledge and understanding of life. Dance is the combined declaration of what I know, understand, feel and express not just with my artistic mind but with the clay that my mind molds. I find that if I go to my sacred space first, my inspiration is already completed in my minds eye. It's like getting a glimpse of a masterpiece before you can physically see it in reality.

As for the veteran dancer and teacher, she looks back at her students with a wise woman's prophetic eye. She can glimpse at their potential, therefore guiding and helping them mold their own masterpieces. This is truly the wise woman's magic, her ability to foresee and be apart of the universal creative process one masterpiece at a time…ceaselessly.

23 - The Split Personality

"We are not retreating - we are advancing in another direction."

General Douglas MacArthur

Meeting dancers is the best part of belly dancing which means associating with dancers professionally, brings in lessons that are essential to understanding our own community. Some women, who have belly danced for awhile, acquire veiled character traits that can be equivalent to the possession of body and soul. Sometimes this possession takes on a dark undertone that reveals itself like a scary movie. At first you think you are imagining something scary, only to find out it's the real deal. As an observer, you can feel like you are looking at someone who is out of a creepy Sci-Fi flick. On the other hand, if the tables are turned, you might find that you are the main attraction, becoming possessed yourself. The end result is a group of unique personalities that are subtle at first, until they become a refined and scrupulous scourge, in other words the split personality is born.

Image-Delusion

Years ago, I met a young woman at a Hafla who told me she had been belly dancing since she was a young child and learned from her mother. I eagerly asked her what style she danced and she told me "Middle Eastern." I said, "I know sweetie, but what style did your mother teach you?" And again she said, "Middle Eastern." So as you can imagine, we kind of went round and round. Third times the charm, right, so I mustered up as much patience as I could and asked again," What style does your mother teach?" Again she said, "Middle Eastern." Just as I was about to pull my hair out, one of my students took her by the arm and said sympathetically to me, "I'll explain it to her for you." Off they went and I thankfully kept my hair or at least was saved from having a bald spot on the top of my head. I realized that there are some women who go through life being uniformed in belly dance and they don't even know it. To say one is a belly dancer can mean more than the actual training itself. This type of personality will look like a dancer and create a whole image, based on her need to be someone else. We can all relate to this because everyday life can become mundane, but there comes a point in time when you have to know the difference between saying one thing and actually doing it.

Hidden Agenda

Being friends with dancers can sometimes feel like walking through a house of mirrors. You don't really know if what you are looking at is real. This is where the personality I call, the *hidden agenda* lurks. It lures you in with a friendly, sweet disposition and before you know it you've been had. The *hidden agenda* personality plays you like a chess game, making sure that it is one move ahead of you. A French proverb says, "You cannot play at chess if you are kind-hearted." So the hidden agenda side tracks you with compliments and well wishes but cunningly uses this strategy to set you up. I prefer card games myself only because it's a little easier to see if someone is cheating.

In regards to the game of belly dance, a couple of years ago I met a dancer who I thought was really nice. We got along really well and I found her to be very accommodating and genuinely passionate about her dancing. As our friendship grew, I told her everything that I was doing in my dance career, bringing her into my confidence. Unfortunately, I came to realize as time past, that I had a big mouth because my ideas became her ideas. The bottom line is, formulating ideas can be a very personal matter, almost like creating a masterpiece. Sometimes friends need to stand back and watch the fruition of ideas come to life. They can then get ideas from the fruits of their friend's labor.

After awhile, it felt like there was an unspoken rivalry between us. It even went to a funny, quirky level when I told her that I was considering breast augmentation. Besides the occasional costume blooper, I was having the surgery done because I had breast fed my daughter years ago, and my breasts were uneven. So my reason for having surgery was to correct this problem. Low and behold before you could say, "Boob job," she had her breasts done. But boob jobs aside, I have to say, I felt like my friend was trying to fit into my self identity and make it apart of hers. What has become a sad reality for me is learning that at times, this art form can become a very lonely endeavor. Trusting other dancers has been a hazard for me but there have been a few saving graces, who are still my dear friends to this day. So the only thing you can do is be aware of dancers who come across obliging but have a hidden agenda to get ahead at all costs, which really means at your cost.

"You don't have to swim faster than the shark. You just have to swim faster than the person you're with. That's what friends are for." Kevin Nealon

Pink Elephants

Big shows can bring the best out in people and definitely the worst. Sometimes, you can watch a person's personality change before your very eyes. I watched this progressively happen through out a show I co-produced with my good friend Rozana al Jinan and another dance friend who was a student of mine. There was a lot of laughter which was a good thing and thankfully the laughter kept us all reasonably sane. This was especially true as we watched the different, dramatic scenarios occur through out the months of preparation and rehearsing. A few dramatic outbursts did occasionally come from me, which surprised me because I had no idea I was so naturally, theatrically inclined.

On one particular evening it was my students turn to be dramatic. I remember our meeting was specifically about props and we where debating about two very large, heavy wooden boxes that represented a library scene in the show. She was adamant that we needed them. So we gave in, but they became monsters on stage and when the show was over, they were the pink elephants in the room. It's funny, how something as simple as a huge prop can suddenly become invisible at day's end. I'm including myself here, because as far as I was concerned after our final bows, they didn't exist in my world.

From Zombie to Hyde

Maybe the Hyde *personality* waits for those specific, opportune times to come out and play, especially when stress is at its peak. It waits for thoughts that are hidden away that normally wouldn't occur due to appropriate behavior. Human nature has a way of escaping the confines of sanity so that the Hyde persona can come out occasionally, to create a little mayhem. More times than not, I became a zombie and was flabbergasted I could play the part so well. Maybe all those old scary black and white films impacted me more than I thought. My preference would have been the Hyde personality because you can at least have some fun while you go insane. The zombie on the other hand, just stands there and stares off into outer space or looks like it's in outer space.

Interestingly enough I did experience a hint of my Hyde personality on one specific occasion. For some odd reason, hours before our show was premiering, the in-house director started to yell at me in front of students, guest dancers and back stage help. I went from zombie to ballistic in zero to sixty seconds and I had to be persuaded to walk away, as I was yelling at her. Isn't it amazing how a good old fashioned finger pointing can help get the message across? I mean pointed here not raised in the ultimate gesture. Case in point, finger pointing has it's moments of equality with giving someone the finger. I call it the Hyde finger.

Denial

This personality seems to be so unassuming at first. It's one of those personalities that doesn't feel like much is going on, until it's too late. I watched helplessly as I was immobilized with these personalities' characteristics such as the state of being oblivious. When drama happens on a regular basis, denial steps in to save the day. It was like I was hypnotized and when the drama unfolded before me, I said nothing until it was all over. After the fact, ten thousand perfect, rhetorical words filled my head which was usually days or weeks after the drama occurred. Right off the bat, denial can give us a speech impediment that won't allow one single word out or for that matter a sentence in the moment we need them the most. The build up of this voiceless phenomenon, would heat up to a boiling point and the drama queen in me occasionally went wacky. Laughter would enter at the oddest of times that had an insane undertone to it because I would giggle walking down the hall, in the middle of a meeting, in the car by myself, in the shower, you get the picture.

Insanity

146

There is an accomplice to denial that evolves along with most any show or production that it is called *insanity*. She is the sister of denial that is sly, cunning and a master in the ways of manipulation and mysterious phobias. The impending event became one of these phobias was like a nervous tick that wouldn't go away. The feeling of always wondering if I was supposed to be somewhere never left me. Driving in my car at times would become a frightening experience, because my heart would palpitate and I would panic out of the blue. It was almost like my body would scare me for fun or as I have rationalized, it was getting even with me for all the stress I put it through. One thing I realized early on, I needed to create an off button. The only problem was, I would forget where I put it and my body and mind had a great time watching me look for it. Yes, for a while there I had 3 personalities, and not all of them were my friends. And just incase you were wondering, I never found my off button.

Hallucination

It's so funny to look back at some of the shows I did, and to see that a very unusual personality somehow snuck its way into my subconscious. At times it seemed to actually, make my life better or I should say slightly delusional. This personality is known as *hallucination*. I would swear I said things to people, only to find out that I didn't. A good example of this was the constant replies back saying, "No, I didn't hear you say that I was supposed to come to the last three rehearsals." Or my favorite was, "You didn't tell me my choreography had to be done by today." So I ask you, where was I in the moments that I thought I was telling people vital information, they needed to know? I must have had an out of body experiences at each and every time I talked to some of the cast and crew. The only one, who remembered what was said, was my co-producer, Rozana, She made me feel better because we were both hallucinating at the same time and experienced the same side effects. I eventually knew something was wrong because I started talking to myself more and more but at least I remembered what I said so that in itself was comforting.

The Ladder of Success

There is no greater joy then to go to a belly dance workshop and to slowly approach the vendor's room full of costumes, jewelry, hip scarves and veils. The pupils dilate, and there's a glazed look over the eyes which indicates that a time warp has just taken place.

I can remember going to my first workshop in my early years, when some dancers took it upon themselves to show me the ropes. The first thing I was taught, perplexed me because it made no sense. I was told that there were certain dancers that you did not approach or talk to unless they talked to you first. With a frown on my face I asked," Why?" They answered back, "They are well known and you are not." How they could be so well known, that you couldn't walk up to them and say hello, I thought to myself. I resisted this idea but resigned myself to the fact that maybe this was the way it was? I finally realized that these ladies were coming from what I call the *ladder of success* mentality.

Years later I was teaching at a local workshop in Albuquerque when a dance acquaintance came up to me and said, "Why are you teaching here?" My first thought was, what a weird question to ask but I answered that I was invited to teach by the workshop sponsor. She then said, "I wonder why?" I laughed at her but was saved by a dancer who came up to me right at the same time, and told me how much she enjoyed my class. I turned to my dance acquaintance and said, "Looks like you don't know what you're missing." We looked at each other for a few seconds before she walked away. Silence is golden they say, but sometimes there can be a lot said with just a look.

For some reason this incident reminded me of the earlier one, because with both incidences each scenario had to do with where a dancer was on the *ladder of success*. The dancer that came up to me had this same personality trait, but with a slightly different twist. She's the type of dancer that judges other dancers according to where she is on the ladder of success. Sometimes if another dancer goes up a step or two, someone like her might feel slighted by a success that is not hers. She'll look at her lack of success as a result of you taking it from her. The dancers, who took me under their wing, lead me to believe that success is only for the chosen few. As for me, I would rather see success and know what it feels like, than to be a dancer who goes around feeling slighted. You can't become successful if you are constantly watching everyone else advance, while you are taking notes.

Self Important-Negotiator

Learning about all the different types of split personalities, is a part of my dance career that is comparative to a class I had to take in high school that I didn't like. The one big difference is, if you forget your lesson at school, you knew what grade you would get. In belly dance, if you forget your lesson the end result can be someone undermining your hard work.

This next split personality, I would have to say is one to look out for because it can negotiate you right out of a performance, workshop or any type of venue. I'm also including into this characteristic a unique type of negotiator that can serve you belly dance in a minimal amount of time called, belly dance to go. This negotiator is unique because they can talk you into taking short cuts, and fly by night classes so you can become a professional dancer in the time span of a few months, instead of years.

The *self important-negotiator* has very unusual characteristics that can elude the sanest person into thinking things about themselves that aren't true. Becoming a director of a show is an intense responsibility but this type of personality will inundate the meaning of your title with nonsense. For instance, in the last show I co-produced, for all intense and purposes I was also the director, but a few people didn't want me as a director so they started to call me the director of paper work, a demeaning jab at my capabilities. It became obvious in a short span of time that being a director just meant that, I was the gofer, the messenger of bad news, and the shoulder for all problems to land on- period. Imagine all the above happening while doing your part in holding the show together. Sometimes, you just have to turn deaf to this kind of personality and go your own way.

I realized that the *self important-negotiator* can't allow anyone else to be their equal, so they create the problem-reaction-solution scenario. This personality, surprisingly and conveniently has the solutions to situations that pop up around them. The problems seem to always affect those around them, except for them. This personality is defined by the problem-reaction-solution characteristic to the point that it is instinctively ingrained in all their business dealings. Dealing with this type of personality is equivalent to cleaning my room, only to have someone come in right behind me and mess it up. The end results of my efforts never amounted to much so I learned quickly that having people around me that I could trust, ensured that I wasn't always cleaning up after myself.

"Self-delusion is pulling in your stomach when you step on the scales."

Paul Sweeney

I learned that not all people I have worked with represented themselves as genuine. Some of what I saw was a façade based on what they wanted me to see. Facing our own image and recognizing who we are can be equivalent to walking into a dark room with the floor moving. In some ways we are all apart of the carnival of life, trying to convince the masses that what they see is real. It is only fitting that at the end of the day, we try to convince even ourselves. Because of this we see the initial beginnings of where split personalities come from; our very dreams and aspirations, illusions, disillusions, and inconsolable disappointments all mixed together creating a toxic fabrication of the self.

Walking the path as a dancer takes the same amount of steps as everyone else; the important thing is not to compare your footprint with others. The split personality can't exist in a happy person who dances for no other reason than just because. This emotion is really a state of mind that is tranquil and relaxed. I wish I could say, I learned this lesson a long time ago, but then I wouldn't have met all the various personalities that made themselves known to me through out the years.

But I have to say in regards to my sanity, my mind isn't so crowded anymore and it's great having only one of me in charge. On second thought, I can only hope there's just one of me in here.

24 - Divas "Legends in Their Own Minds"

A Diva is not color blind to cultures, she is color enhanced so she can celebrate the differences."

Personally, I don't think there is one person who reads this chapter title who won't be able to hold in a giggle. We have all come across this type of personality through out our journeys. I have actually seen a variety of Divas, and to be honest, I was a bit envious of their crowns which lead me to secretly try one on myself. I didn't know a throne came with the crown and I realized for the most part, nobody really noticed or cared where I placed my throne. Realistically, carrying around a thrown and wearing a crown gets tiring, plus there's the need to defend the throne, making sure nobody tries to take it over. Needless to say, I ended up tossing both throne and crown deciding I was better off without them.

Luggage Diva

There are some dancers who take their position in life very seriously, and for the most part, they deserve to be respected. But sometimes, the expectations of these dancers can be overwhelming. Interestingly enough, for some strange reason there seems to be a connection between Divas and luggage. It so happened, I was picking up a dance acquaintance, who was teaching a workshop in Fort Worth, Texas when this mysterious phenomenon first surfaced. I had another dance friend with me, who was a very well known dancer in her own right. Just as the luggage was being wheeled to my car, I witnessed them looking at each other, neither willing to budge an inch, to pick up a suitcase. It was almost like a stand off, to see who could wait the longest and not budge. With a huff and a puff, I ended up putting the suitcases in the car by myself. By the time I was done, the stand off had diminished into smiles and light hearted talk. There was apart of me that felt a little peeved and left out because I didn't get to partake in the stand off, but I reasoned with myself, my time would come.

The Blown Luggage Diva Moment

It's funny how people view Divas and even funnier how their personalities change from dancer to devotee. I witnessed this at a workshop, I taught at years ago. I was one of 3 teachers asked to come in for a weekend workshop, so I was excited to say the least. When I arrived at the hotel, there was a group of dancers, waiting in the lobby to greet me. I walked into the hotel with my luggage in tow, but was pleasantly surprised when one of the girls asked if she could take my luggage for me. I told her no, that I was fine, but in the back of my mind I thought I should have taken her up on her offer. Thinking nothing more about it, I went to my room to rest and relax before the other teachers arrived. A little later, I came down to the lobby just in time, to greet one of the teachers who had just arrived. As she got out of the car, she asked which of the girls was bringing in her luggage. There were many dancers outside waiting to greet her and they all flocked to her suitcases, bringing them in behind her. It was a funny sight to witness, because I exaggerate you not, they all gathered around her luggage like grateful groupies and adoring fans. Not only did they take her luggage into the hotel, but all the way up to her room. The following day, I was talking to some of the same girls about various belly dance topics, when the conversation abruptly changed to Divas. A few of the girls told me something that really surprised me. They told me that I was too nice, and that I should behave more like a Diva. So it occurred to me, right then and there, I had blown another luggage Diva moment!

It's Just a Name

One way of knowing if someone is a Diva, is by the sheer number of people they have around them, who are their subjects. It's amazing how Divas can get anyone to do anything for them, at a moments notice. There are many reasons for the devotee state of mind, it's the grass looks greener on the other side mentality that does more harm then good. It's always better to water your own grass and make it grow, instead of tending to someone else's lawn. I realized a long time ago, that just because someone can dance better than me, doesn't mean they are happier then me. I finally got over the cultist mentality, when I took my rose colored glasses off and realized, I was ignoring my own needs. In addition, I was focusing on people who had entirely different philosophies than me, and I couldn't ignore the differences anymore. I just call this growing up and maturing.

It's important to see accomplished dancers but we have to find similarities, so we can see the connection we have with each other. This connection means we are all human beings with varying talents, the only difference being how we grasp the various opportunities shown to us. It's what we do with the opportunities of life that separates us from each other. Those who understand and grab hold of opportunities focus on their path, creating success. Those who watch others become successful either follow along their footsteps or covet a success they feel they can never achieve.

This brings to mind a student that use to come to my classes when I had my studio years ago. In the beginning, I remember her telling everyone how proud she was to be apart of my studio. She would bring me soft drinks all the time without me asking her to. When I would offer her money, she would insist that she bought them because she wanted to and didn't want any money. This kind of obligation was uncomfortable after awhile, so I started insisting on giving her money and then eventually had to ask her to stop bringing drinks altogether. The expense was unnecessary since students would bring their own. Eventually she started showing up to beginner classes wanting to help me with students and finally, she insisted on finding venues for the studio, which I was grateful for. But it wasn't long after she started to help me out, she started to complain to students that I was asking for help all the time and that I wasn't paying her for it. This all happened within a 5 month time span and towards the end of her stay, I was happy to see her and her problems go. I was a Diva in her mind for only a short period of time, but I realized that being "her" Diva, was a set up. If we don't personally own our invisible crowns, those who give them to us, will be inclined to take them off, at the slightest hint of disappointment.

There are always consequences to being crowned by someone else's expectations. I have had the name Diva given to me more times than I can count, through out the years. The removal of the crown just comes with the territory or as I have found, stems from an individuals issues and problems that have nothing to do with me.

The Wannabe Diva

There is a funny kind of behind the scenes mania that happens to women who catch the Diva bug. There really is no sense to it or short cuts because when it's all said and done, women know if they are or aren't in the presence of a Diva. But there are always those few who feel it necessary to push the envelope and try the crown on before their time. The feeling is like trying on your mother's shoes and jewelry for the first time; it's kind of exciting and mischievous at the same time. As little girls, we know our time will eventually come. The *Wannabe Diva* will do anything to either buy the title or falsely proclaim it as hers. One tactic is by hanging out with Divas. She can be hazardous because her eye is usually on someone else's crown.

The first time I ever encountered a *Wannabe Diva* was back in Dallas, when I was performing at a restaurant. A dancer came in to check out the restaurant, and I just happened to be the dancer performing that evening. She was a pretty, curvaceous woman with long blond hair and a loud laugh. I took a liking to her immediately, and sat down with her after my show was over to chat with her. As soon as I sat down, she started to tell me about her great talents as a belly dancer. She told me she lived in the Middle East when she was growing up, and that the Arabs just loved her dancing. She did such a good sales job of selling herself that even the owner of the restaurant came over and sat down. Within a short period of time, he decided to have her come in to audition. Even though I had never seen her dance, I was totally convinced she was top notch. The following Friday, she came in to audition, surrounded by her family, who were her loyal entourage. I had assumed there would be loyal fans clamoring to come in to see her perform, but nobody else showed up.

The moment her music started, her whole family held their breath as if Isis herself was sashaying onto the stage. Once she was on stage, she started to dance with her veil, doing the same movements over and over again for the entire song. Seriously, it was as if she was stuck on repeat. When the next song came on, she again continued to dance with her veil, doing slightly different moves, yet similar as before. The restaurant owner nudged me and asked me to come back to the kitchen with him. I didn't want to go because I just knew she was going to let that veil go and do something awesome. So I told him I would go back to the kitchen later, after her performance. He nudged me again and emphatically said, "Now!" So I got up a little embarrassed and walked into the kitchen with him. As soon as I walked through the doors, he grabbed my arm and asked me, "What are you trying to do to me?" I was like a deer caught in the headlights because I knew he was speaking English but it made no sense to me. I said, "What are you talking about?" He said, "You said she was a great dancer and I have her come here to audition and she is terrible, just terrible!" I just about flipped my wig and looked at him in disbelief saying, "You, thought she was great because she spoke so highly of herself. It's not my fault you don't like her." He was banging pots and pans around because he was mad and I left the kitchen in a huff because I felt like I was being blamed for something that wasn't my fault.

As I sat back down, she was in the middle of doing a sword dance and it seemed to me as if she wasn't really dancing, she was just moving enough not to be stationary. When her drum solo came up, I realized that this dancer had not only duped the owner but me too. I ended up sitting in my chair waiting for a great performance that never happened. When she finished, her family applauded and yelled her name as she bowed before them. She was acting as if she had just performed the dance of the seven veils.

The owner was nowhere to be seen at this point, and the family was going on and on about her performance, as if she was a super star. I found it amusing that the mother wouldn't speak to me the entire evening, even though she knew I also danced at the restaurant. The evening was all about her daughter, and it finally became clear why this gal, thought so highly of herself. Needless to say, you can imagine her reaction at the end of the evening, when the owner told her that she wouldn't work out. She was in disbelief and for a minute, she just stood there in silence, as if it didn't compute. She ended up leaving in tears, with her family obviously upset and angry. They didn't bother to say good bye, as they rushed out of the restaurant. I sat back at the owners table and had a glass of wine with him. Neither one of us said anything to the other, there wasn't any need.

The Maleficent Diva

I have to admit that Walt Disney knew a lot about Divas. If you look at the wonderful cartoons of Cinderella, Snow White and Sleeping Beauty just to name a few, there is always a villainess waiting for some misfortune to happen to the main character. I always wondered why he chose older, angry women to emulate evil queens. Now that I am older, I kind of look at the story lines a little differently. I find that with each story there are common elements with the queens; jealousy, envy, vanity and the age denial dilemma. So my next question is, why portray these elements in women and not men?

Is it that Hollywood stereotyped us with these characteristics or can there be 1some truth here? There is no better way for us to find out if this is true, then

153

to experience shows, haflas and workshops so we can find out for ourselves. The answer lies with each experience we have and the women who cross our paths. Sometimes, the wind blows someone in our direction that has very eccentric tastes and opinions, especially about the world that evolves around them. Eventually, this type of person emerges, waiting for the right moment to show herself because the *maleficent diva* can't stay hidden for long. This particular diva is like a scorpion or snake because they strike when you least expect it. I always resemble a rabbit when I come across this type of Diva. My ears twitch and my eyes bulge out slightly and I have the strongest desire to run. The problem is that this type of person always seems to know just before you are going to high tale it out of there because they go back to hiding their true selves. It's baffling because I'll think I'm seeing the beginnings of someone starting to become possessed and then all of a sudden they turn back into a normal person.

I am usually left bewildered, wondering if I saw what I think I saw.

Self Deserving Diva

With this dance form there seems to be a specific type of personality that I occasionally come across in shows, haflas or workshops. Truthfully to a certain extent, it's a personality trait that we all have, but with some people, it seems to be more prevalent. I remember a funny experience years ago, when I witnessed this type of Diva. It all had to do with the seating arrangements at a workshop show. There was a line of chairs that were being kept for a group of dancers, and the dancer holding the chairs, would not let anyone sit down, within the entire row. Dancers were getting mad and the drama was hysterical. I was one of the unfortunate individuals chased off my chair with the dancer on my heels shrieking behind me that the chairs were taken. Finally her teacher arrived, along with her entourage and nobody had a clue about who they were. I was expecting a super star, and there in front of me, was a group of dancers just like me, except they had better seats and view of the stage. Right then and there I decided that I was going to hog whatever chair I decided to sit on at any future show or venue. At that moment, I realized, I was starting to become just as self serving as the group in front of me, but I rationalized to myself that at least I would have a better seat!

Okay, maybe the above experience wasn't exactly what I was talking about regarding the *self serving diva*. It did have similar elements to it, but what I am really talking about is a little more calculating. It's a type of manipulative maneuvering that can affect unsuspecting dancers in a multitude of ways. For me, this type of personality is harder to understand because you are dealing with someone who doesn't care what the outcome is, except for them.

I lost out on a gig in Mexico City, because of a well known dancer, who decided at the last minute she wanted to continue performing at a club that was hiring me for the same position. I was actually driving to my travel agent, at the very moment, when I got the phone call telling me, I was unceremoniously out of a job. What bothered me the most about this situation was, the people who contacted me, told me that they were tired of this particular dancer's antics and wanted her replaced. Who knows what happened, maybe I was used as a bargaining chip. All I know is that it sucked big time losing a gig to this type of personality.

Woe is Me Diva

Easily the w*oe is me Diva* could be apart of most women's make up, and I must be honest here, because I not only know this one well, but I can act this one out perfectly to within an Oscar winning performance. Basically, I have definite dramatic and emotional attributes, that come in handy on stage, but they tag along with me off stage. I just thank God that I have the stage as an outlet, because otherwise, I would be a raving lunatic. Let's be fair here, because there are many reasons to be a w*oe is me Diva,* especially in the entertainment business. The problem with this type of Diva is when it becomes a constant state of being. I think this is one of those Diva personalities that creeps up on women, and before they know it, it's knocking at their door. It waltzes in with an effortless glide that has everybody dancing to its tantalizing tune, without anyone being the wiser.

This type of personality can be associated with behind the scene productions, and shows or interaction with other dancers. It's really about how women relate to the world around them based on how they feel about themselves. We tend to see life in a way that validates our relationship within ourselves and the insecure issues that bond the two together. However, there can be a darker side to this personality, because it doesn't question itself; it questions the world around it. It's the day to day validation that makes this personality dig its heels in deeper; wallowing in its own distorted validation.

It's almost like putting on glasses that only allow you to see the world only one way. The damage here is not what the world does to us; it's what we continually allow ourselves to see, so we can keep validating the same problems over and over again. The only way to stay out of the grasp of this personality is to realize that what we attract to us, is connected to how we feel about ourselves. The end result of both these elements in situations is either the chance to get past our own issues and free ourselves, or to stay stagnate in our self imposed impression of how we are treated by others. Sometimes we attract to us the same scenarios over and over again. If we step back from the situation, we can usually see what is going on and know we have choices. This type of personality alludes to the false presumption that they have no choice or say in the outcome of their lessons. In the end, it has always been about stepping up to the plate and realizing that choices have always been there, as habitual people sometimes we choose not to see them.

Gossip Diva

This particular Diva is probably one of the most destructive of them all, because there is usually, no positive outcome intended. The ultimate agenda of the *gossip*

155

Diva is to purposely undermine another person. Most of us know this one well being in the entertainment business. With gossip, it's easier for people believe in what they are told without looking for the truth. They see the answers in the half truths that are being told to them. In the case of the last show I co-produced, we found that gossip affected one of the actors in our play who quit on us out of the blue. This was a great example of someone making a judgment call based on half truths, instead of finding out the facts. The *gossip*

Diva in the end got the result she wanted. The quote, "With friends like that, who needs enemies" speaks volumes here!

Another aspect of gossip is the fact that it lingers in the mind like a viral contagion. Let me clarify the differences in how a normal person would react to stress, versus stress from a *gossip Diva*. There is a natural stress button that when pushed too much, will overload on a normal person. The *gossip Diva* will look at a normal person's stress levels and make sure their stress button gets pushed to a breaking point, even if she has to push it herself. It's best to figure out who your friends are before hand, so you can stay in your safe zone. Pretty much try and figure out who the *gossip Diva's* are and stay clear of them.

The Feminine Diva

The definition of a Diva is either a distinguished woman singer or a successful woman performer. So there is a definite link to the name and the entertainment business. But it is definitely a misused word that as you have read in this chapter can be connected to negative connotations. It's important for me to clarify the power and strength this word not only carries with it, but what it really represents.

Years ago when I was studying to be a medicine woman, I was surrounded by women who venerated their bodies in a way that allowed for life to happen naturally. As I moved and traveled around, I lost contact with these women and my self awareness and body acceptance slipped away as the months turned into years. One amazing woman in particular, who I have known since I was 19, is my mentor Ana. She is a healer and a priestess of the ancient ways who taught me and prepared me for the ways of a "Sage." She always told me it didn't matter how young a woman was, there was always a sage inside her that needed mentoring. Even though these words have stayed with me all these years, I find I really miss the self assuredness Ana and my women friend's possessed, because in the world around me, I have found less and less of it. I had no idea how lucky I was to not only know Ana but to learn from her our feminine sacred ways. The traits she passes on are elements sacred to the *Feminine Diva*. Ana embodies and teaches, acceptance of self and knowing ones own body, valuing relationships, compassion for others and extending a hand in friendship, no matter what anyone's story might be. A Diva is not color blind to cultures, she is color enhanced so she can celebrate the differences. These teachings can be found even in belly dance and this is why I believe it is so attractive to

156

women; it's an ancient calling from hundreds of years ago, referred to as, the Silk Road of life.

One interesting aspect of the *Feminine Diva* is that she believes in, *female equality*. The creative aspect of what we do tends to tip the scales of this attribute in a world where we gauge what we do according to what others are doing. The *Feminine Diva* sees all creative efforts as equal, yet knowing that the level of experience for each dancer will vary. It's not about the beginner dancer versus the master dancer; it's about being in an environment that nurtures everyone's needs. The problem becomes a segregation mentality that is permeating our dance world and has for a long time. The creative aspect of what we do seems to make us judge others in our world harsher then the average woman on the street.

The *Feminine Diva* isn't hard to find, because every woman is born with these attributes. We isolate ourselves by looking for outside validation, then wonder why we are so lost. The saying, *"everywhere you go there you are"* is a wake up call reminding us, we are never alone. The *Feminine Diva* resides in a place where she not only knows herself but is satisfied to be within her own company. I guess this is apart of what I miss, women who are content to be themselves, without comparing their uniqueness to others. I am constantly striving to recapture this quality that for some unknown reason eludes me, yet it is always within reach.

The flow and ebb of life happens whether I am aware of myself or not. I don't want to allow life to happen according to my limitations because it would become stagnant. As I look back at my life, it has become amazingly clear to me that what I miss most about the *Feminine* Divas who were in my life years ago, is they were the perfect personification of the ebb and flow of life. It was the harmony they emulated and the creative synergy they shared with me that constantly reminds me of what I can become and who I really am, the "Feminine Diva."

25 - Being a Happy Belly Dancer Without Being a Super Star

"Sometimes just feeling good is what it's all about, nothing more and nothing less."

I felt this particular subject was noteworthy enough to talk about, because of a very human and devious subconscious voice that speaks to all of us , saying…*what if.* It's like we have a little person on our shoulders saying, we could be the next super star; miracles do happen. It's not like I haven't heard women say they belly dance for themselves, but eventually, thoughts of fame and fortune intertwine themselves with everyday reality.

When I see women take workshops, I wonder if they secretly wish they were the ones teaching the class, perhaps it's an innate desire to become that which seems out of ones grasp. It's considered an honor and a declaration of success to teach workshops, the ultimate achievement of a dancer. I have been asked to teach workshops and it's great feeling to be apart of the teaching process. Does this mean I've made it? I really don't know but I don't stay up at night worrying about it. It's all in the mind of the beholder.

There has to be talent, right? I mean who could possibly become famous without being talented, beautiful and established especially in our business? Maybe I'm being a bit sarcastic here, but we all know this isn't always the case, because I have seen well known dancers who were blown out of the water by unknown dancers, in shows. I have seen troupes that were just amazing that I haven't heard of before, and as an entertainer I have come away from shows realizing that in any type of entertainment business, determination added with talent has a lot to do with getting ahead. One show can make all the difference with backstage buzz. Obviously, there has to be a specific drive to get on the ball to rise above the rest, while pushing the envelope of panache and expectations. People won't go out of their way to follow you around or hire you unless they think you are a success already. If you are the kind of dancer waiting for horns to blare and carolers to sing you the answer, then you will be waiting for your next big break, till the cows come home.

There seems to be a pastime of *don't tell,* that allows for dance acquaintances and friends to stand aside and watch other dance friends flounder and hesitate in their career choices. It's like if we all drown together then it's not so bad sinking. There is also a competitive instinct that dancers have with each other, where they secretly desire each other's downfall. Even friends don't always cheer for each other to succeed, especially if they are focusing on the same level of success. But for some reason, being the artists, and creators of inspiration that we are, there seems to be an intense need to be accepted and to be told so. I don't think any of the other arts are any different because my ex-husband was a well known painter and it was the same within his world of canvas, oils and competitive egos. When artists put apart of themselves out in the world to be judged or viewed, there seems to be a vulnerability that makes them a little more sensitive and neurotic. Not everyone has it in them to become a dancer, sculpture or painter but the ones who are born with the calling, endure a life time of creative impatience. It's the sensitivity to the creative process that makes the performer or artist more acute and aware of life and pain. And I can tell you for a fact that artists are the practiced thespians of their own sorrows, because they wallow in them. Even to this day it's hard for me to admit this because sometimes I walk through the front door covered in my own issues.

Introspection is an interesting thing to experience because it brings out our thoughts that we put away on the shelf called undisclosed. One boxed up topic that I took off my shelf, is the fear of failure. It can become an old tattered dress that when worn quietly says, "*Who the Hell am I?*" As entertainers it's a legit question that haunts us all. In the end the answer or its legitimacy can only be comprehended by each dancer's understanding of how she travelled her path.

I think it really comes down to what belly dance gives to each individual dancer that allows them to cope with their life's path. Decisions are impressed upon women differently than men, because we are conditioned by outside influences in different ways. There seems to be a war between what we know is right and what we know doesn't hold water. But what is really interesting, is the fact we will give sustenance to something that is pushed upon us by outside influences. This esthetics war was never ours to begin with, yet we participate by default. We bring in remnants of this battle that rages inside us into our dance and personal lives. Sometimes this conundrum motivates and inspires women to create interesting choreographies but the end result is still based on issues that are manipulated towards women.

How we deal with these influences trickles down into our personalities, values, expressions and movement. It's like seeing the view of the world in each dancer's choreography yet none of them show the same issues the same way.

"The thing that is really hard, and really amazing, is giving up on being perfect and beginning the work of becoming yourself."

Anna Quindlen

After years of dance, I finally realized that back bone is really the strength of a person's convictions and values. I found out that not only did I have back bone, but I also have an Italian instinct for survival that came in handy when I was at my wits end. Looking back at my dance career, it became apparent there had to be a separation from my perception of how I think people view me versus how I see myself. I had a tendency of assuming people saw me as incompetent, and I was always going the extra mile to show them I was the consummate professional. Experienced dancers not only know what needs to be done, but they have an acute understanding of problem solving with precise timing. Towards the end of producing multiple shows, I had developed a calm demeanor that masked the turmoil going on inside me.

I no longer needed to prove myself, because the feeling of accomplishment with the relief of a long journeys end, taught me well. In my eyes I was successful, and I had come full circle to where my dreams and aspirations first dwelled. Erica Jong's quote, *"Everyone has talent. What is rare is the courage to follow the talent to the dark place where it leads,"* resonates with me because the journey of dance isn't marked like the yellow brick road. It can be scary and challenge the most sure footed traveler. I realized that in walking my path, I became oblivious to the obvious, my belly dance image completely merged into me, and we finally became one. It was such a subtle change, that I didn't notice it at first, but ultimately I felt her in me because she made herself known. This had always been my ultimate goal, but I thought it would happen when I was a lot older. The fact that the merging took place just after the last show I co-produced, lead me to believe I had come full circle. Our journey can be so full of *"dancing"* that we forget to stop and see where we are.

Maturing with our dance helps us stand up for ourselves, knowing that our dance is written and recorded according to our own description. If we sell our dancing to the highest bidder without foreseeing the consequences, then we set ourselves up for unexpected disappointments that can be costly. Allowing someone else to be responsible for our dreams creates a powerless feeling. We have to make sure our dreams thrive and live in the safety of our choosing. Making sure each goal arrives in one piece strengthens our foundation so that our dance image not only comes to life but that our desires have somewhere to grow. Working towards aspirations of fame and fortune means more, especially when it grows from seedlings that are nurtured from our own efforts. When the end results come to fruition, there is no greater pride then to know we made it happen through will power, intention and an unwavering desire to succeed. They are apart of the nutrients of the Universe that grow, visually satisfying us with the best results.

Once I saw what I wanted from my career, it started to make more sense to me. I started looking at where I was and I began to enjoy my career for what it was giving me. In doing this, I was able to stay focused on goals that mattered to me and make them come true. I found being happy started to matter more then being famous, and that my fear of silently disappearing through the quicksand of life, was bogus. Being distinctively who I am, with no apology was the ultimate goal which made me irreplaceable. Yes, in the end, the lesson I learned is and always has been that we are irreplaceable because we create from our own inspiration. But I have to say, that occasional insecurities come back to haunt me and I am faced with reminding myself that with all experiences, I am constantly growing. The ego goes into hiding and every so often peaks out in the most inopportune times.

160

When we live in constant fear and frustration of what we haven't done, then we can't appreciate who we are and what we have accomplished in the moment. Each moment lost can add up to weeks, months, years that start to feel like centuries. Self appreciation is a key element in my life as a dancer now, and it is the measuring stick I use to gauge what is best for me. In the past, I use to force myself to be happy with projects I was doing, because I was trying to convince myself that I was where I wanted to be. Negotiating happiness isn't and shouldn't be an option for anyone. With certain experiences, I learned that when I bartered with my happiness the end result was paying with my health.

Happiness is more then a cure, it's a way of living life and enjoying every minute of it without regret. A dancer on stage performing for the pure joy of it is more then an accomplished dancer, she is a women content with herself. This is power in itself and why as dancers our journeys ultimately lead us back to ourselves, better, happier women living in our bliss which ultimately means we become our own Super Star as bright as the shiniest star.

6 - Learning to Accept Your Sage Years

"Because I am a woman, I must make unusual efforts to succeed. If I fail, no one will say, "She doesn't have what it takes"; they will say, "Women don't have what it takes." Clare Boothe Luce

These last few years I have found that I am not as immortal as I thought I was. All of a sudden, out of the blue, I became a human furnace, waking up in the middle of the night drenched in sweat. My body decided to go into pre-menopause and she didn't feel the need to give me a heads up. Since no one in my family has gone through this change of life, I found I am pretty much on my own. As a dancer this was almost catastrophic (yes, I am being dramatic) because even with all the exercise I was doing, the weight wouldn't come off. I found that teaching weekly dance classes, making twenty year olds sweat wasn't taking the weight off either and this included limiting my bread and sugar intake. Even with all I was doing, I didn't see much of a difference and when I actually had a trainer and went to see her once a week, the daily exercise to-do list seemed to be hours of working out. The weight came off but I was miserable with my daily workout schedule, and found that while I did feel better, my attitude was getting worse. I thought to myself, I am a dancer, this shouldn't be happening to me! But happening it was and this is now my new reality.

Vanity does play a huge roll in dance and even though this is an uncomfortable thought, it unfortunately is the truth. I didn't realize how comfortable and friendly I had become with such a nemesis. My vanity has been taking a beating and deep down inside, I know it isn't such a bad thing, because life is the teacher of humility. I also took for granted that my imaginary *Fairy Godmother* would always make me look younger, defying my actual age. At this point she is missing in action!

Just like nature has her seasons our bodies have their own, and vanity can't exist in a world that follows nature's guidelines: Vanity, after all is the illusion of how we see ourselves; our perfections versus our imperfections. I have found that I am now in a position to help pave the way for older dancers because I am in a position of seeing this dance form from a different vantage point, even though it's taking time to get used to. The opportunities that I took for granted years ago are no longer a choice for me, but I am not brooding, because my options are different now and in many ways more rewarding.

The journey getting to where I am at this moment has been rocky and unpredictable. I had to understand that my footing had to be solid before I could take the next step, and if I blindly stepped forward, the saying "bottoms up" took on a whole new meaning. It isn't that I traveled through dangerous terrain through out my career; I didn't always follow my gut. I believe in taking leaps of faith occasionally, just like the next person, but sometimes I landed in situations that I wasn't prepared to handle. There is nothing like experience being the teacher, but I have to admit, I wasn't always the best pupil. Ignorance isn't always bliss, especially when we find ourselves in situations where we are calling the shots. In this business, there are always a select few who will make those in charge, pay for calling the shots. I now understand why experienced dancers prefer to come in and perform in shows. They know from experience, letting someone else call the shots allows them the joy of performing. Experience isn't the bitch here; she is the refined dancer that has learned her lessons well. The innocent fun and passionate emotions that started me off on my belly dance journey have turned into a blinder free perspective of my dance path. Learning the hard knocks of my path has made me wiser in choosing my battles. Today, I am a more peaceful warrior with a few battle scars. This doesn't mean I don't trip myself up occasionally, but I know how to pick myself up and keep on walking.

The age old question of how old is too old is a debatable issue for me, because I have always felt that women who keep their age a secret, keep those dastardly double standards alive. I think women don't know they are apart of a hypothetical time warp, created not from birth but by proxy. Who decided women couldn't or shouldn't say their age. Why the secret? We have a culture that naively thinks that over the hill is descriptive only to women. It's interesting how age has dictated the dos and don'ts of women in society. As women, is it in our inherent history to listen and follow codes of behavior long withstanding or do we become deaf to an unrealistic dictum that was never ours?

Even in our business there will never be a coalition for older dancers, because younger dancers are too busy working to worry about becoming the older dancers. As women we have to take a good look at how we contribute to the age old issue and decide how we want to change our image and ideals for future generations. Since I have a daughter and niece, I want them to represent a new generation of women who aren't concerned with age at all. The best way I can help this happen is to celebrate each year I am alive, and acknowledge not just my age to society, but the change in my views on tradition. If I stand strong as a woman, then my age doesn't really matter. We are not our age, we are a combination of lessons learned, not learned and repeated. Age will always catch up to us no matter how much we hide from it so it's easier to embrace it. If we can teach the younger generation to look age square in the face then they will have a better chance of reflecting change back to society. But the biggest flaw women have, is they magnify ten fold what they fear the most in their reflections. Releasing memories that magnify these flaws allows all of us to see not only ourselves but other women clearer and without the blemish of our fears or societies dictates.

After so many years of living the belly dance dream, I have come to a place of appreciation for having had the conviction and perseverance to walk on the road less travelled. But sometimes even in doing something that we love, it can become like a runaway train. I didn't say train wreck, because that hasn't been my experience but there has been more times then I care to remember where I was going down hill and it felt like I didn't have any brakes. It has been in those moments where I hurt the most that I learned the most, which ultimately helped me overcome any disillusionment within myself and dance. By combining different philosophies in life, I learned that it's never what others do to us in life that scars us the most but the relationship we have or don't have with ourselves.

"There is in every true woman's heart, a spark of heavenly fire, which lies dormant in the broad daylight of prosperity, but which kindles up and beams and blazes in the dark hour of adversity." Washington Irving

Something that amazes me even to this day is the fact that the Universe silently watches me, giving me a helping hand when I need it most. By accepting life's reprieve I became apart of making my goals successfully happen along with fate. The difference now is that I take my time on my path knowing that each experience will come in its own time. The best part about being where I am is knowing there are no buttons or off switches to be pushed, unless I create them. Keeping the impulse to go against the flow of life at times can be a challenge because of old habits. It's because of these old habits that an off switch even exits. It has always perplexed me why I would want to create something that screws me up in the first place.

Within our lives as dancers we affect the connection we have with our dance form by accepting who we are as women and feeling comfortable with what we see in the mirror. This is where the duality of the two comes together, and we dance from a place of freedom. It's not about the audience or the applause; it's about us coming in and placing ourselves where we belong in the eternal circle of life. The *"Divine Unrest"* sets in motion the first baby steps we take as dancers and it never leaves us, until the fires of creativity burn out or the inspiration fades away to dust. I was born a dancer and I will die a dancer.

As a Norman Cousins quote states quite well, ***"Death is not the greatest loss in life. The greatest loss is what dies inside us while we live."***

The End for now………..

Additional Resources

Here's a list of other Belly Dance resources you can click on and check out.

- [Online Belly Dance Classes w/Leyla at Belly Dance Village](#)
- [More Belly Dancing Articles on Leylas Blog](#)
- [Belly Dancing Leyla Style Mobile App](#) – On Amazon for Android
- Belly Dancing Leyla Style Mobile App on [iTunes for iPhone and iPad](#)
- Belly Dancing Leyla Style Mobile App on [Google Play](#)

Made in the USA
Lexington, KY
21 April 2013